HOME OFFICE RESEARCH STUDY

Trends in crime and their interpretation

A study of recorded crime in post war England and Wales

by Simon Field

A HOME OFFICE
RESEARCH AND PLANNING UNIT
REPORT

LONDON: HMSO

© *Crown copyright 1990*
First published 1990

ISBN 0 11 340994 X

HOME OFFICE RESEARCH STUDIES

"Home Office Research Studies" comprise reports on research undertaken in the Home Office to assist in the exercise of its administrative functions, and for the information of the judicature, the services for which the Home Secretary has responsibility (direct or indirect) and the general public.

On the last pages of this report are listed titles already published in this series, in the preceding series Studies in the Causes of Delinquency and the Treatment of Offenders, and in the series of Research and Planning Unit Papers.

Her Majesty's Stationery Office

Standing order service

Placing a standing order with HMSO BOOKS enables a customer to receive other titles in this series automatically as published.

This saves time, trouble and expense of placing individual orders and avoids the problem of knowing when to do so.

For details please write to HMSO BOOKS (PC13A/1), Publications Centre, PO Box 276, London SW8 5DT and quoting reference 25.08.011.

The standing order service also enables customers to receive automatically as published all material of their choice which additionally saves extensive catalogue research. The scope and selectivity of the service has been extended by new techniques, and there are more than 3,500 classifications to choose from. A special leaflet describing the service in detail may be obtained on request.

Foreword

An understanding of trends in crime is central both to Home Office policy and to criminological research. While recorded crime has grown substantially since the last war, its rate of growth has fluctuated greatly, for reasons which have not always been clear. Amongst other findings, this research study shows that a large part of this volatility can be attributed to the cyclical behaviour of the national economy.

This result is of considerable practical and theoretical value. Figures for recorded crime become more meaningful when their volatility can be understood in relation to prevailing economic circumstances. Moreover, to the extent that the national economy is predictable, trends in crime may also be so, representing a useful means of forecasting the basic component of demand on the criminal justice system. More fundamentally, the finding also suggests that the economic circumstances of individuals play a role in the causation of crime.

ROGER TARLING
Head of the Research and Planning Unit

Acknowledgements

A number of people provided commments and suggestions in the course of this research project. Outside the Home Office, particular thanks should go to Professor Ron Smith of Birbeck College and to Christine Godfrey of the University of York, both of whom contributed very helpful technical advice. Within the Home Office I received helpful advice from a large number of people, including Anne Barber, Lawrence Davidoff, Lizanne Dowds, Jean Goose, Chris Lewis, Joy Mott, Pat Mayhew, Chris Nuttall, John Siraut, Roger Tarling and Peter Ward. I am grateful to them all.

SIMON FIELD

Contents

	Page
Foreword	iii
Acknowledgements	iv
Chapter 1 Introduction	1
Chapter 2 Methodology	11
Chapter 3 The results and their interpretation	18
Chapter 4 Conclusion: Implications of the findings	54
Appendix A The regression results	60
Appendix B The data	74
References	81

1 Introduction

This report describes a study of trends in crime in England and Wales during the post-war period. The study was designed to explore the range of factors, particularly economic factors, believed to be related to crime.

The study employs statistical techniques whose presentation is necessarily somewhat technical. These more technical aspects are addressed in chapter two covering the methodology, and chapter three which describes the statistical analysis and interpretation of the data. This introductory chapter describes the approach which was followed and summarises the main results, while the final chapter, chapter four, discusses the implications of the research findings.

The analysis of trends in crime, as with any similar series of data, is a complex technical and theoretical task. To demonstrate a statistical relationship, it is not enough to show that two factors show trends in the same direction; this could easily be pure coincidence. Instead the revelation of a more subtle interconnection of patterns over time is required. Moreover, in analysing patterns over time, it is also necessary to take into account the possibility that a causal factor will have an impact on crime only after a delay, and the level of crime itself is likely to influence the level of crime at a later date.

Econometrics is a branch of statistics which has been designed to grapple with these dynamic relationships. It has been developed primarily by economists who have a particular interest in changes over time in sets of interwoven economic variables—such as interest rates, exchange rates, unemployment and economic growth. The field of econometrics has developed rapidly over the last two or three decades, and the tools are now readily available with which to tackle statistical time series such as those for recorded crime.

The idea that crime may have economic causes has a long history. Criminologists writing during the last century such as Von Mayr (1867) Poletti (1882), Ferri (1900), and Bonger (1916) all discussed the issue and described relevant statistical evidence. In more recent times a large number of studies have given attention to unemployment, but have also examined other economic factors such as income and inequality; (see reviews of the literature by Orsagh and Witte (1981), Long and Witte (1981) and Box (1987)).

The common thread which unites much of the discussion of crime and the economy is the idea that wealth in society may represent both an incentive and disincentive to property crime. It is an incentive in that, with wealth, there are more goods to steal, and a disincentive in that wealthy people have less need to steal. A large part of the theoretical literature on the relation between economic conditions and crime consists of an elaboration of these two basic ideas.

However the double effect of wealth on crime makes theory difficult to test—at least in aggregate data. It can be argued both that an increase in social wealth should cause crime to rise, and that it should cause crime to fall. If theory is here ambiguous in its implications, then so have been the recent empirical findings, which have shown ambiguous evidence for a relation between unemployment and income levels of crime, although some more consistent evidence of a positive relation of inequality and crime; (Box, 1987; Long and Witte, 1981; Orsagh and Witte, 1981.)

Most of the recent time series studies of recorded crime and its correlates are based on data from the United States and are reviewed in the three publications just mentioned. In Britain Wolpin's (1978) study is the major previous time series study of crime in England and Wales. He presents results for the 1894-1967 period. He reports some association over time between criminal justice variables, the numbers of young men, unemployment and crime. However it is far from clear that Wolpin's study would withstand modern statistical assessment. A study by Brenner (1976) has been subject to some methodological criticism (see Orsagh and Witte, 1981).

Recording and reporting

This study is based on crimes recorded by the police; many crimes, however, are not reported, and some reported crimes are not recorded. According to the 1988 British Crime Survey, 10 per cent of all incidents of vandalism were ultimately recorded by the police, 21 per cent of woundings, 41 per cent of burglaries and 86 per cent of thefts of vehicles (Mayhew, Elliott and Dowds, 1989). Figures for recorded crime therefore measure reporting and recording practices as well as actual crime. This raises the question of the extent to which trends in recorded crime reflect trends in recording and reporting rather than trends in actual crime.

The most direct evidence on this topic comes from the long time series comparison of victim survey and recorded crime data in the United States. Annual data for the period since 1973 indicate that the annual growth of most types of actual crime (as measured by the victim survey) is highly correlated with the annual growth of recorded crime. This result is reassuring from the viewpoint of the present study, for it implies that factors related to trends in recorded crime may also be taken to be related to trends in actual crime.

To give a practical example of what this might mean—suppose that recorded crime grows more slowly; by five per cent one year, eight per cent the next year, and three per cent the third year. Actual crime meanwhile grows by four per cent the first year, seven per cent the next, and two per cent the year after. In this example the growth rates of actual and recorded crime are highly correlated, and fluctuations in the growth rate of recorded crime therefore imply fluctuations in

INTRODUCTION

the growth rate of actual crime. Overlaid on this association is a long run increase in the proportion of crime that is recorded, by about one per cent a year.

In the analysis conducted here, the problem of recording and reporting effects was tackled directly. In searching for an explanation for fluctuations in the level of recorded crime, factors examined included both those believed to be related to the level of crime, and those which are believed to be connected with the reporting and recording of crime. Little evidence in fact emerged that fluctuations in the annual growth of recorded crime are related to recording and reporting factors, a result consistent with the evidence from the United States.

Long run and short run effects

Economists who analyse the behaviour of national economies have become accustomed to the idea that factors with a dominant influence in the short run behaviour of the economy can play only a marginal role in the long run, when very different factors assume prominence. For example the exchange rate and interest rates have great influence on the level of economic growth over a period of a year or two, but over a period of decades increases in productivity through the application of technology, and the level and development of skills in the labour force will be much more important factors at work. The ebb and flow of the business cycle has to be distinguished from long-term currents in economic activity. (Another example lies in the distinction of meteorology from climatology: very different factors are relevant depending on whether we are forecasting the weather for the weekend, or predicting the climate a century from now).

Many economic time series therefore show a distinctive pattern. In most industrialised countries, including the UK, economies have grown at a steady long run rate over the post-war period, with only small fluctuations from decade to decade. Quite sharp fluctuations however, occur from year to year as economies swing from boom to recession. Many other economic variables, such as real (after inflation) growth, income and expenditure, show a similar pattern over time as overall economic growth, since they are closely connected with the latter.

Recorded crime rates display a pattern over time which is similar in type to that of these economic variables; crime growth varies substantially from year to year, but not very much from decade to decade. Post-war growth in crime is summarised on table 1.

The striking feature of this table is its consistency. For each of the twelve categories of crime, for each of the four time periods the level of crime grew (except for sexual offences which were static during the 1970-79 period). Moreover ten of the twelve types of crime showed positive rates of growth in single figures during the whole period, the exceptions being criminal damage and theft of vehicles.

TRENDS IN CRIME AND THEIR INTERPRETATION

There are variations. We might note the relatively high rates of growth for vehicle offences (which now represent about one quarter of all notifiable offences) and the relatively low rates of growth of sexual offences. Vehicle crime shows high rates of growth in the 1950's, but substantial reductions thereafter, perhaps because of better vehicle security, or because there are now so many cars that further increases do not increase the opportunities available to steal them. While these variations deserve interpretation, they do not detract from a striking picture of consistent long-run growth in crimes whose origins are diverse.

Table 1
Rates of growth in recorded crime
Average annual percentage growth rates over stated periods.

	1950-59	1960-68	1970-79	1980-87	Whole period (1950-87)
Residential burglary	3	9	3	8	6
Non-residential burglary	4	8	2	4	5
Theft from person	2	7	12	3	6
Shop theft	5	9	8	2	6
Theft of vehicle	16	5	8	3	10
Theft from vehicle	10	10	5	11	8
Other theft	3	6	2	2	3
Robbery	7	10	7	12	9
Violence against person	10	9	9	5	9
Sexual offences	5	2	0	2	2
Criminal damage	9	12	24	12	14
Fraud	2	6	5	2	4

This long-run consistency is in striking contrast to the year by year pattern, which shows sharp fluctuations. For example, thefts of vehicles grew by 25 per cent in 1974 but by only five per cent in 1975. Burglary from a dwelling fell by 10 per cent in 1973 only to rise by 23 per cent in 1974.

The similarity in general pattern over time between crime and economic factors gives rise to two ideas which underlie the analysis developed in this research study. First, crime, like the economy, may be subject to strong short term influences which are very different from its long term determinants. Second, one explanation for the similarity in pattern could be that economic factors are one of the major causes of crime.

INTRODUCTION

A summary of results

Consumption and crime

The main finding of this study is that economic factors have a major influence on trends in both property and personal crime 'Personal consumption *per capita*' is the amount that each person in the country spends, on average, during the year. 'Real' (after inflation) annual growth in personal consumption was found to be inversely related to growth in recorded property crime. Thus in years when people are increasing their spending very little—or even reducing it, property crime tends to grow relatively quickly, whereas during years when people are rapidly increasing their expenditure, property crime tends to grow less rapidly or even fall. In England and Wales, the relationship has held throughout the 20th century, and has been particularly strong in the last twenty years. (See figures 1 and 2 in chapter two) A similar association between property crime and personal consumption can be demonstrated for the United States, Japan and France in the last 15 or 20 years, but is not apparent in Sweden, and the relationship takes a different form in West Germany. Economic factors in general, and consumption growth in particular, appear to be among the most important determinants of fluctuations in the growth of property crime in industrialised countries.

The evidence suggests that this effect is *short term,* rather than one which might explain the growth of property crime in the long term. Thus although property crime certainly tends to grow less quickly during years in which consumption grows rapidly, there is also evidence of compensating 'bounce-back' in the following years. Thus the long term rate of property crime growth might be unaffected by a surge in consumption growth. While the full relation between long-run economic growth and growth in property crime is as yet unclear, it seems that the effects identified in this study have only a limited bearing on the issue.

Personal crime—sexual offences and violence against the person (but not robbery)—also shows a distinctive relation to personal consumption. It appears to increase in line with consumption, so that personal crime appears to increase more rapidly during periods of rapidly increasing consumption. This means that personal crime responds to consumption growth in the *opposite* manner to that of property crime: during periods of slow consumption growth, personal crime tends to grow more slowly than usual, whereas in periods of rapid consumption growth, personal crime also tends to grow more rapidly.

These results provide a powerful explanatory framework against which trends in recorded crime can be assessed, and offer an immediate insight into the trends in recorded crime in England and Wales during the 1980's. The most striking feature of these trends has been the way in which during the first years of the decade in 1980 and 1981, recorded property crime of most types grew very rapidly, while personal crime grew very little. There followed a gradual reverse in this pattern, such that personal crime grew rapidly in 1987 and 1988, while property crime grew very little during the same period. This shift can now be attributed at least in part to the underlying effect of the business cycle: personal consumption actually fell during the 1980-81 recession—so that a high rate of property crime growth and low rate of personal crime growth might have been expected. Consumption grew extremely fast in 1987-88 underlying the observed reverse pattern of low (or negative) property crime growth and rapid growth in personal crime. Similar patterns are observable in previous economic cycles.

Explaining the relation between crime and economic cycles.

In principle, consumption growth might have three sorts of effect on crime:—

(i) It increases the goods available for theft or vandalism: the opportunity effect.

(ii) Consumption growth indicates an increasing capacity for the lawful acquisition of goods, thereby reducing the temptation of unlawful acquisition through theft: the motivation effect.

(iii) It alters the pattern of crime opportunities by precipitating an alteration in lifestyle or 'routine activities': the lifestyle effect.

Here it is argued that property crime is primarily affected by the second 'motivation' factor in the short run, so that rapid growth in consumption generates low growth in property crime. In the long run the other two factors appear to balance out the motivation effect, so that the long run effect of economic growth on property crime may be small.

Why does only one factor dominate in the short run? Potential victims are very widely spread in society. Potential offenders however, are likely to be concentrated in particular social groups, whose position in the labour market is liable to be weak or marginal. Fluctuations in aggregate consumption growth will therefore tend to be amplified in the experience of potential offenders, since marginal labour market groups commonly experience aggregate fluctuations in such an amplified form. Better placed labour market groups tend to be more insulated from the vicissitudes of the economy. It follows that a surge in consumption growth will be amplified in the experience of potential offenders, and the 'motivation' effect on them will therefore outweigh the 'opportunity' and 'routine activity' effects on potential victims. Property crime will therefore be lower than it otherwise would be. Conversely a deep trough in consumption growth will result in more property crime. In addition, a sharp fall in consumption growth may trigger frustration as economic expectations are lowered. This could undermine social controls.

This theory provides an explanation of the observed relation of consumption and property crime, and explains why the effect is cyclical rather than long term.

Personal crime, in the form of violence against the person and sexual offences, responds positively to rapid consumption growth. Personal crime is not directly affected by the goods available to the victim or the offender, but is affected by the pattern of routine activities, which in turn is affected by consumption and income growth. There is good evidence that people who go out more often are much more likely to be the victims of personal crime than those who do not, and there is also evidence that when consumption increases some of that consumption goes on increased time spent outside the home. This suggests an explanation for the observed positive relation between personal crime and consumption: when spending rises, people spend more time outside the home, and as a result there are more opportunities for personal crime.

Unemployment and crime

The idea that unemployment causes crime has long been discussed in criminology. Unemployment rises and falls over the business cycle. In the face of the powerful evidence of a relation between crime and the business cycle, what role can be attributed to unemployment?

(Offences of violence against the person turned out to have a distinctive relation with unemployment, which will be discussed separately.)

Although personal consumption and unemployment are both indicators of the business cycle, they behave somewhat differently; in particular, fluctuations in unemployment tend to lag behind consumption growth. As described, fluctuations in consumption growth are coincident with fluctuations in the growth of property crime. It is therefore no surprise that in practice, trends in personal consumption are tied much more closely to crime trends than are trends in unemployment. Once the effect of personal consumption on crime is taken into account, no evidence emerged, despite extensive statistical testing, that unemployment adds anything extra to the explanation of any type of crime. The whole relation between the business cycle and crime appears to be encapsulated in that between personal consumption and crime. Thus fluctuations in the total number of unemployed persons appear to be independent of fluctuations in the number of offences.

Both the power and limitations of this result deserve emphasis. A major drawback of many of the published time series studies of unemployment and crime is that unemployment is often the only economic indicator which has been used. As it has been demonstrated here that crime does have a strong relationship to the behaviour of the economy, it will be no surprise that some relation emerges when unemployment—alone of economic indicators—is compared with crime rates over time. The data used for the current study shows such a relationship. The strength of the analysis conducted here is that it demonstrates an extremely strong relationship between crime and the business cycle, and demonstrates that unemployment adds nothing to the explanation of this pattern, once consumption growth—the key factor—is taken into account. It follows from this result that any simplistic theory of the aggregate relationship between unemployment and crime—for example one that claimed that for every extra 10 unemployed persons there would be one extra offence per year—must be counted as disproved.

TRENDS IN CRIME AND THEIR INTERPRETATION

The qualification to this result is that it refers to aggregate data. Even if trends in national levels of unemployment are unrelated to trends in national levels of crime, it does not follow that unemployment cannot cause crime. For a potential or actual offender, the experience of unemployment might precipitate offending or an increase in offending. An increase in the rate of unemployment among this population sub-group will therefore increase the rate of offending by this sub-group. However as potential and actual offenders are unlikely to have a labour market position representative of the population as a whole, fluctuations in the rate of unemployment among this group may follow a very different pattern from fluctuations in the national rate of unemployment. It follows that fluctuations in aggregate unemployment could be independent of fluctuations in crime, even though unemployment is causing crime.

Violence against the person, beer consumption and unemployment

Violence against the person was found to be strongly related to the level of beer consumption, although not to other forms of alcohol consumption, or with the number of on-and off-licences. The implication of this finding is that while alcohol as such is not a cause of violence against the person, a particular combination of alcohol and social circumstances — perhaps young men drinking a lot of beer in pubs and clubs — is conducive to crime of this type.

Violence against the person, like the other 'personal' crime of sexual offences seems to rise in response to rapid consumption growth. While general consumption is correlated with beer consumption, the effect of general consumption was separately identifiable from that of beer consumption. Uniquely amongst crime, violence against the person is strongly related to unemployment during the preceding year and is also affected by the level of unemployment benefit. This strongly suggests that unemployment — perhaps long term unemployment in particular — and the material deprivation that goes with it, may be a casual factor in crimes of violence against the person. During economic boom periods therefore, the positive effect of rapid consumption growth on violence against the person is subject to a countervailing influence — the decline in unemployment which tends to occur at such periods. This apparent paradox is probably explained by the heterogeneous nature of the 'violence against the person' category: it includes offences which range from domestic violence to pub brawls, whose causal basis will be diverse.

Crime and demography

Young persons are more likely to become involved in crime than older persons, and men are more likely than women to take part in crime. It follows that the level of crime at any place and time will depend not only on the size of the population, but also on the proportion of young males within that population. Over time this proportion can change significantly, reflecting trends in fertility

INTRODUCTION

and the knock-on effects of fluctuations in the size of the preceding generation. Trends in crime should therefore reflect changes in the numbers of persons in the age and sex groups most prone to crime. This principle underlies the long term projections of crime and the criminal justice system which are made by the Home Office from time to time.

Direct confirmation for this demographic effect emerged from this study. Growth in the number of young men was found to be positively related to growth in all types of crime with the exception of robbery. Similar results have been obtained from research studies conducted in the United States.

Apart from the direct, arithmetic effect of changes in the size of the age and sex groups most prone to crime, such demographic changes may have other social impacts which result in changes to the crime rate. One theory suggests that when the number of young people increases more rapidly than the whole population, the opportunities for social advancement open to those young people in a variety of different arenas will often not be able to expand to meet the demand. This reduction in lawful opportunities may increase the temptation to become involved in crime.

Some evidence in support of this hypothesis emerged from the study, as rates of some sorts of crime—notably shop theft and criminal damage—appeared to respond to changes in the size of age cohorts to a greater extent than could be explained by the purely arithmetic, direct effect.

Interaction between crimes of different types

There is every reason to expect that crime of one sort will be related to crime of other sorts. Some people may start on a life of offending on one sort of crime, and then 'graduate' onto more specialised or more serious types. Fluctuations in one type of crime may therefore signal a kind of early warning of fluctuations in another. Alternatively, when crimes of one type become more difficult, and the level of this sort of crime falls, potential offenders 'displace' their attention onto more vulnerable targets, and the crime rate for this other sort of target rises as a result.

An exploratory examination of these effects was undertaken. First, *unexpected* fluctuations in the growth of crime were isolated. These fluctuations were unexpected in the sense that they deviated from trend rates of growth, and could not be explained by the set of factors described above. These unexpected fluctuations were then compared with unexpected fluctuations in the growth of other kinds of crime during the following year, to see if a statistical relationship could be identified. A variety of relationships between the different sorts of crimes were suggested by the evidence, but the statistical techniques used to assess these relationships require further refinement before the evidence can be regarded as final.

TRENDS IN CRIME AND THEIR INTERPRETATION

Criminal justice factors

Criminal justice system factors were also examined, including the prison population, the clear-up rate and the number of offenders guilty or cautioned. These factors had a patchy relationship to crime. The number of offenders found guilty or cautioned tended to have a positive relationship to growth in crime during the following year, so no deterrent effect could be inferred. However growth in police strength (manpower) was found to be negatively related to theft of and from the vehicle, other theft and sexual offences. This may imply some deterrent effect of police strength. Fluctuations in police strength were positively related to fluctuations in the growth of offences of violence against the person — probably a recording effect.

Other factors

A range of other potential factors were examined, and some of them were found to be associated with trends in crime. The findings included the following:

Growth in the number of live births was positively related to growth in residential and non-residential burglary, and robbery during the following year, and to growth in shop theft in the year after. This may be attributable to the economic impact of the birth of children on their parents.

2 Methodology

The data for recorded crime

The study was conducted on annual data for recorded crime in England and Wales since 1950. Total recorded notifiable crime was disaggregated into twelve categories as follows:—

1. Residential burglary.
2. Non-residential burglary.
3. Theft from the person.
4. Theft from a shop.
5. Theft of a vehicle.
6. Theft from a vehicle.
7. Other theft (i.e. thefts other than 3-6 above).
8. Robbery.
9. Violence against the person.
10. Sexual offences.
11. Criminal damage.
12. Fraud.

The precise definitions of these variables are given in Appendix B.

The variables were selected and constructed in an attempt to cover most types of notifiable crime, and to ensure that the time series were as consistent as possible. In establishing the series, account was taken of the definitional changes which have affected the series. The most important of these changes were the 1968 Theft Act, which changed the basis of many theft and burglary offences, and the changes in counting rules implemented since 1980. In addition, there have been some less important changes in legislation and in local recording procedures of which it is not possible to take specific account.

TRENDS IN CRIME AND THEIR INTERPRETATION

Table 2
Effects of the 1968 Theft Act on the data series.
Numbers of recorded offences before and after implementaiton of the Theft Act.

	1968	1969 figure (following implementation of the Theft Act)
Residential burglary	85000 (housebreaking)	181800 (burglary in a dwelling)
Non-residential burglary	127000 (shopbreaking)	233100 (burglary not in a dwelling)
Theft from the person	8650	81700
Theft from a shop	78500	91200
Theft of vehicle	21300	137600
Theft from vehicle	188700	176300
Other theft	529100	498200

The effects of the 1968 Theft Act on the data series are illustrated in table 2. The legislation had a large effect on recorded cases of vehicle theft, and a lesser but still very substantial effect on the classification of burglary offences. For other crimes the effects are much less evident. However the effects of this change on the analysis is less than might be immediately thought, since (for reasons discussed below) the analysis dealt with annual growth rates rather than absolute levels of crime. Clearly the growth rates for 1968-69 are distorted, and to resolve this problem the growth rates for this year were estimated as the arithmetic mean of the growth rates for 1967-68 and that for 1969-70, and these estimates used in the analysis. This is a relatively crude procedure, but it only affects one year in the sample out of about 35, and was backed up by inserting a dummy variable for 1969 into the model, a procedure which identifies and removes any distorting effects resulting from any oddity in the 1968-69 data. (The dummy was subsequently removed if it appeared to be irrelevant.) A more serious difficulty is the possibility that the changed composition of the crime categories will result in different patterns and trends in the pre-1969 data in comparison with the period since 1969. This possibility was eventually assessed by splitting the data series at 1969 and using structural stability tests to compare the two sub-periods. However, given that, as it turns out, the growth of most types of property crime has broadly similar underlying determinants, we can have some confidence that changes in the composition of a property crime category should not have drastic effects on the trends in the data series. The 1980 changes in the counting rules were similarly dealt with using a dummy independent variable for 1980.

Explanatory factors

A range of potential factors affecting recorded crime rates were assessed. These factors can be classified as follows.

(i) Economic factors.
(ii) Demographic factors.
(iii) Criminal justice factors potentially affecting either the level of crime or its propensity to be recorded.
(iv) Other environmental factors potentially affecting crime.
(v) Other factors potentially affecting the propensity for crime to be recorded.
(vi) Other variables, including dummy variables for particular years in which definitions of crime and counting rules were changed, and a time trend variable.

The variables and the reasons for their inclusion in the model will be described in turn. Full details of the data and its sources are given in Appendix B.

(i) Economic factors.

There is an extensive literature on the potential relation of *unemployment* to crime and so a measure of this was included. A connected argument has been that poverty causes crime, and to measure this, the real level of *unemployment benefit* was included. Theories of the economics of crime generally stress both the positive effect of returns from crime and the negative effect of legitimate earnings. Virtually all aggregate economic indicators measure both the availability of goods to steal and the competing returns from paid work. *Real personal consumption per capita*—the amount of personal spending per person was chosen to indicate both.

Other commentators have stressed the importance of available opportunities in the determination of crime. In the case of theft of and from vehicles, data is available on the *number of licensed cars,* and the *number of new registrations.*

On a slightly different tack, the birth of children has a major economic impact on parents, many of whom are in the age-groups most prone to crime. For this reason the *number of live births* was included.

(ii) Demographic factors.

Given the wealth of evidence that young men are over-represented in crime, variables for the four five year age-groups from 11 to 30 for the *population of young men* were included.

TRENDS IN CRIME AND THEIR INTERPRETATION

(iii) Criminal justice factors.

The criminal justice system may affect crime either by acting as a deterrent, or by preventing offenders from continuing to offend by custodial or other supervisory treatment. Variables concerned with the criminal justice system were included in the model to assess such potential effects. *Police strength* may operate as a deterrent to crime, and could also have an effect on recording practice. The *clear-up rate* and *number of offenders found guilty or cautioned* are potential indicators of the risk of apprehension, and therefore of deterrence. The *prison population* may indicate the number of offenders who are in no position to re-offend.

A potential problem with criminal justice factors is that they may both affect crime and be affected by it. This problem is discussed below in relation to the specification procedure.

(iv) Other environmental factors potentially affecting crime.

Alcohol is frequently cited as a potential cause of crime. *Beer consumption* was included as a potential measure of alcohol consumption among young men. There is good evidence that the pattern of leisure activity has an effect on crime. In particular, those who go out more often are more likely to be victims of most sorts of crime. One influence on such activity is the *weather,* and a measure of good weather was therefore included, defined as the annual ratio of the hours of sunshine to the amount of rain.

(v) Other factors potentially affecting the propensity for crime to be recorded.

Telephone ownership makes the reporting of crimes easier, and is frequently cited as a reason for the increased reporting of crimes. Burglary and theft *insurance* policies frequently require the policy holder to report crimes to the police. Measures of *household expenditure on insurance* (which also gives an indication of the potential returns from burglary) and *percentage of households recording expenditure on insurance* were also included.

(vi) Other variables.

Given the changes in crime categories introduced in the 1968 Theft Act, and the changes in the counting rules following 1980, dummy variables were introduced to identify the effects of these changes. A logarithmic time trend variable was included to identify any steady time trends in the data not explained by any of the factors mentioned above.

The regression method

The aim of the exercise was to identify the effect of the whole range of different factors on the level of recorded crime. The technique chosen was regression. In a linear regression model, it is assumed that one variable—the 'dependent' variable—is affected by a set of other 'independent' variables. It is also assumed that the dependence takes the form of a linear equation. On this assumption, and a number of other statistical pre-conditions, estimates can be derived for the relationships of the different independent variables to the dependent variable. The method estimates *all* the relationships taking account of all the others. Moreover the procedure also indicates the reliability of these estimates, so that we have an idea of whether an estimated relationship reflects a real connection, or simply a coincidental feature of the data.

As stated, a set of statistical assumptions underlie the linear regression model and the inferences which are derived from it. They are described systematically in Spanos (1986). These assumptions include that of normality, independence, homoscedasticity, linearity, structural stability and exogeneity. Only recently has it become accepted that these assumptions need to be rigorously tested. In the past these assumptions have not always received the attention they deserve. Wolpin (1978) for example, simply quoted the Durbin-Watson statistic as a test for independence, and this was the sole test conducted. Recent years have seen the development of a systematic set of 'mis-specification tests' covering most of the assumptions. The final regressions quoted here were all tested for independence, normality, functional form, homoscedasticity and structural stability, and the test statistics quoted. These tests are described in Appendix A. The tests are in effect first order tests of the reliability of the regression model itself, as opposed to the second order tests on individual coefficients in the regression results. These first order mis-specification tests assess the reliability of the assumptions on which the second order tests are based.

The issue of simultaneity

The criminal justice system almost certainly has an effect on the level of crime, and for this reason criminal justice indicators have been included in the model. The level of crime, however, also has an impact on the criminal justice system. A surge in the crime rate may result in the deployment of more criminal justice resources, or a change in the proportion of crime which is recorded or an increase in punitiveness. When a standard regression model is developed in which one or other of the independent variables is in fact causally affected by the dependent variable, (for example the criminal justice system being affected by crime) one of the assumptions (that of exogeneity) underpinning the statistical inferences drawn from the regression is rendered invalid. (Spanos, 1986). For these reasons some previous analysts of cross-sectional data have used simultaneous equations to model the interaction between crime and the criminal justice system (Carr-Hill and Stern, 1979). In a simultaneous estimation procedure, a whole set of equations will be estimated together, so that one equation can represent the effect of the criminal justice system and other factors on crime, while other equations indicate the impact of crime on different parts of the criminal justice system.

To avoid the complexity generated by this approach, lagged values of some criminal justice variables were used, since we can be sure that the current level of crime has no causal impact on past values of criminal justice variables. One year (and longer) lags were used for the prison population, the number guilty and cautioned and clear-up rates. Current levels of police strength were used as an independent variable on the grounds that they may be considered as exogenous; decisions may be made to increase police manpower as a result of increases in crime, but it seems unlikely that the time taken to collate crime data, realise that crime is on an upward trend, decide on, and obtain funds for extra recruitment, and actually recruit more police, will take less than one year. Current levels of crime therefore affect police strength in future years, but not in the current year.

The disadvantage of the approach which has been followed is that it may omit causally relevant factors—namely the current level of those found guilty and cautioned, the clear-up rate, and the prison population. As a result the model could suffer from missing variable bias in its estimation. Set against this are the methodological difficulties of the simultaneous formulation. In order to estimate a simultaneous model it is necessary to pick out factors (in advance of empirical analysis) which influence one or the other of crime and the criminal justice system, but not both. In the absence of such factors the simultaneous equation system is not soluble, or 'identifiable' in the terms of the econometrician. Specifying such factors in a non-arbitrary manner is not easy.

The specification procedure.

As described in the opening chapter, the pattern of growth in crime is one of relative stability in the long run growth rate of crime, with substantial short term fluctuations. This suggests a regression model in which the growth rate is the dependent variable, and deviations from a long-run equilibrium growth rate are explained by the different independent variables.

The growth rates for all variables were constructed logarithmically, by subtracting the logarithm of the variable in the preceding year from its logarithm in the current year. This generates a logarithmic growth rate, which for small growth rates is very close to an absolute growth rate (the percentage growth rate divided by 100).

Direct support for a growth rate model was obtained from exploratory regressions conducted in terms of the logarithm of the level of crime. In these regressions the lagged dependent variable was found to have an estimated coefficient close to unity. The model took the form

$$Yt = a + bYt(-1) + Xt'C + Ut$$

where "Yt" is the crime variable, "a" a constant, and "Xt'C" represents (in vector notation) the set of independent variables and their coefficients. "Ut" is white noise. By a simple transformation, since b is close to unity, and since $Yt - Y(t-1)$ is the logarithmic growth rate.

$$Yt - bY(t-1) = Yt - Y(t-1) = DYt = a + Xt'C + Ut.$$

Where "DYt" is the logarithmic growth rate of Y. In effect the regression model in levels, when the coefficient on the first lag of the dependent variable is unity, is exactly equivalent to a model in which the growth rate is the dependent variable.

METHODOLOGY

Twelve regression models were constructed—one for each of the twelve types of crime covered by the analysis. The dependent variable in each case was the growth rate of recorded crime and the independent variables were selected from the range described above, also used as annual growth rates.

The procedures used to develop the final regression model were as follows.

(i) The first estimated model was general, including all relevant variables and one lag on the dependent variable. Variables with t-statistics less than unity were then discarded. All current and lagged relevant variables were then tested and entered or re-included in the model if they had a t-statistic greater than unity.

(ii) The model was re-specified in the light of any mis-specification revealed in the diagnostics. This procedure generated the first stage regressions quoted in tables A.1 to A.12 in Appendix A; the residuals from this stage of the analysis were saved.

(iii) Lagged residuals from other models were tested for inclusion in the model. The regressors were then limited to all and only those variables where the null hypothesis that the coefficient on the variable is zero is rejected at the five percent level. The relevance of additional regressors, dropped at earlier stages in the specification procedure is checked once more. This procedure generated the final regressions quoted in tables A.1 to A.12. Mis-specification tests were conducted, including structural stability tests based on a split of the sample period into two sub-periods before and after 1969.

3 The results and their interpretation

The results of the analysis are quoted in tables A.1 to A.12 in Appendix A. Most of the final regressions appeared to be well-specified. However the following mis-specification tests were failed at the five per cent. level of significance.

Theft from the person: functional form and homoscedasticity.

Theft of the vehicle: predictive failure.

Violence against the person: coefficient stability.

Criminal damage: predictive failure.

All other mis-specification tests for all other types of crime were passed. On the system of equations as a whole therefore, 72 mis-specification tests were applied of which five were failed and 67 passed. It is worth noting that if all the equations are well-specified we would nevertheless expect random error to generate roughly three or four failures in the mis-specification tests, compared with the five which actually occurred (if the null hypothesis of correct specification is valid, one in twenty tests conducted at the five per cent. significance level may be expected to fail). We may therefore regard the equation system as a whole and statistical inferences drawn from it, as reasonably reliable. That said, some caution should be exercised with results from the regressions for theft from the person which failed two tests, and the theft of the vehicle equation, where the evidence of structural instability probably reflects the change in the basis of the data from 1969 onwards.

An extremely important principle must guide the interpretation of these results. Interpretation is not independent of the specification procedure. In this case the specification procedure involved the inclusion of a very wide variety of potential explanatory variables which were then excluded if no statistical relationship significant at the five per cent. level emerged. Such a procedure inevitably contains a significant risk that some of the variables will be wrongly included in the model, because in such a large number of variables some coincidental correlations will inevitably emerge. Some of the variables included in the final model may therefore be spurious. Interpretation of the results has been guided by this consideration in two ways. First, the main findings discussed here rest on patterns across the whole system of equations, rather than on individual estimated coefficients in individual regressions. Second, in cases where weight is

THE RESULTS AND THEIR INTERPRETATION

placed on individual coefficients, it is because they explain a substantial proportion of the variance in the dependent variable, rather than achieving bare statistical significance as a relevant factor. The main examples of the latter approach lie in the discussion of unemployment and beer consumption in relation to crimes of violence against the person.

Crime and consumption

Throughout the post-war period consumption growth has almost exactly mirrored the growth of property crime. In order to illustrate this inverse relation vividly, in figure 1 consumption growth has been inverted to take the form of 'consumption decline' (the negative of consumption growth). A scaling alteration has also been made to the consumption variable.

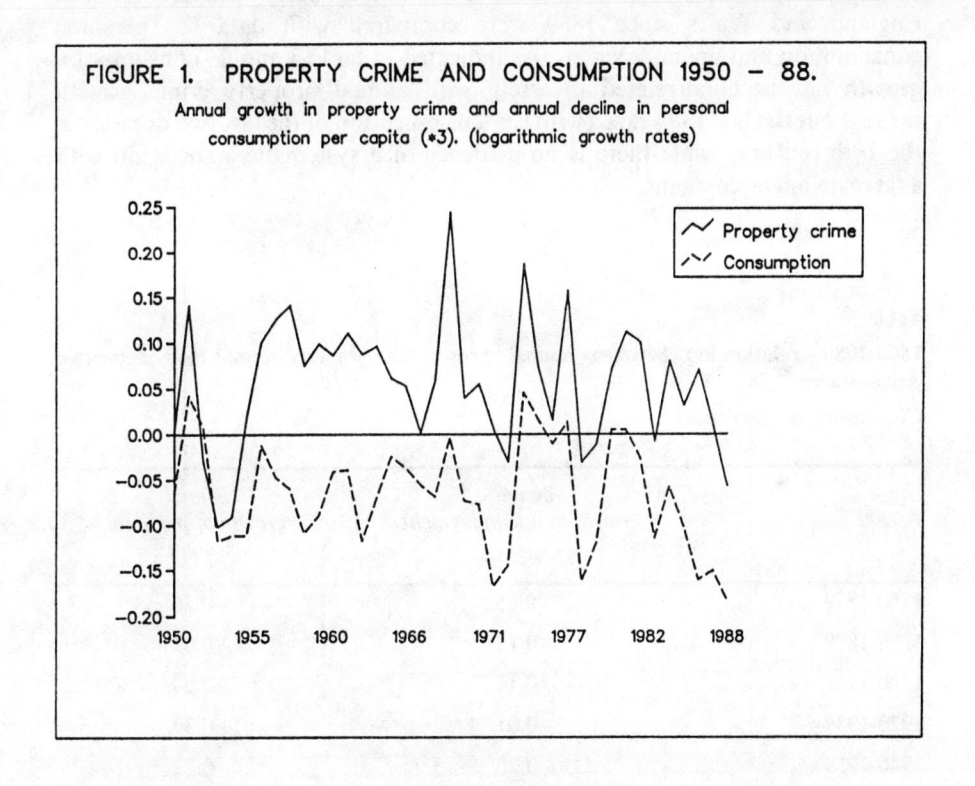

FIGURE 1. PROPERTY CRIME AND CONSUMPTION 1950 – 88.
Annual growth in property crime and annual decline in personal consumption per capita (*3). (logarithmic growth rates)

TRENDS IN CRIME AND THEIR INTERPRETATION

The relationship is so strong that the last two decades of British economic history are in effect written into the history of recorded crime during the same period, with each peak and trough in the economy being accurately mirrored by a trough and a peak in the growth of crime undertaken for gain.

This offers some immediate insights into recent crime trends and the likely future. During the last two decades there have been falls in property crime in 1972-73, 1978-79, 1983 and 1988. Each of these troughs in property crime growth has been broadly coincident with peaks in consumption growth. The boom in consumption during 1987-88, such that consumption growth during 1988 reached a post-war record, appears to explain a large part, if not necessarily all, of the decline in recorded property crime during 1987-88.

Crime and consumption across time and place

Given the strength of the relationship between crime and consumption in post-war England and Wales, an attempt was made to determine how widely the result could be generalised across time and place. Historical data for property crime in England and Wales since 1860 were compared with data for personal consumption and unemployment. As indicated in table 3 annual consumption growth has been correlated inversely with annual property crime growth throughout the last 130 years, (with the sole exception of the last two decades of the 19th century) while there is no evidence of a systematic association with aggregate unemployment.

Table 3
1860-1980: relationship between annual growth in property crime and economic circumstances
Correlation coefficients.

Period	annual growth of unemployment	annual growth of personal consumption
1860-1879	0.65	−0.26
1880-1899	−0.18	0.02
1900-1919	0.16	−0.54
1920-1939	−0.01	−0.39
1940-1959	−0.20	−0.22
1960-1979	−0.09	−0.59

THE RESULTS AND THEIR INTERPRETATION

A correlation table such as this is somewhat crude procedure, since it might simply indicate that there are time trends in opposite directions in the growth of personal consumption and the growth of property crime. A more convincing demonstration of the relation is a simple graph of growth in personal consumption and growth in property crime for the first half of the 20th century leading up to the second world war.

Given the strength of the relation between recorded crime growth and consumption growth in England and Wales, a similar result may be expected to obtain in other countries. With this in mind, data for recorded crime and real personal consumption were examined for the United States, France, West Germany, Japan and Sweden. (Details of the international data are given in appendix B.) In each case the crime variable consists primarily of property crimes such as theft and burglary. Simple autoregressive models were established, yielding the following results.

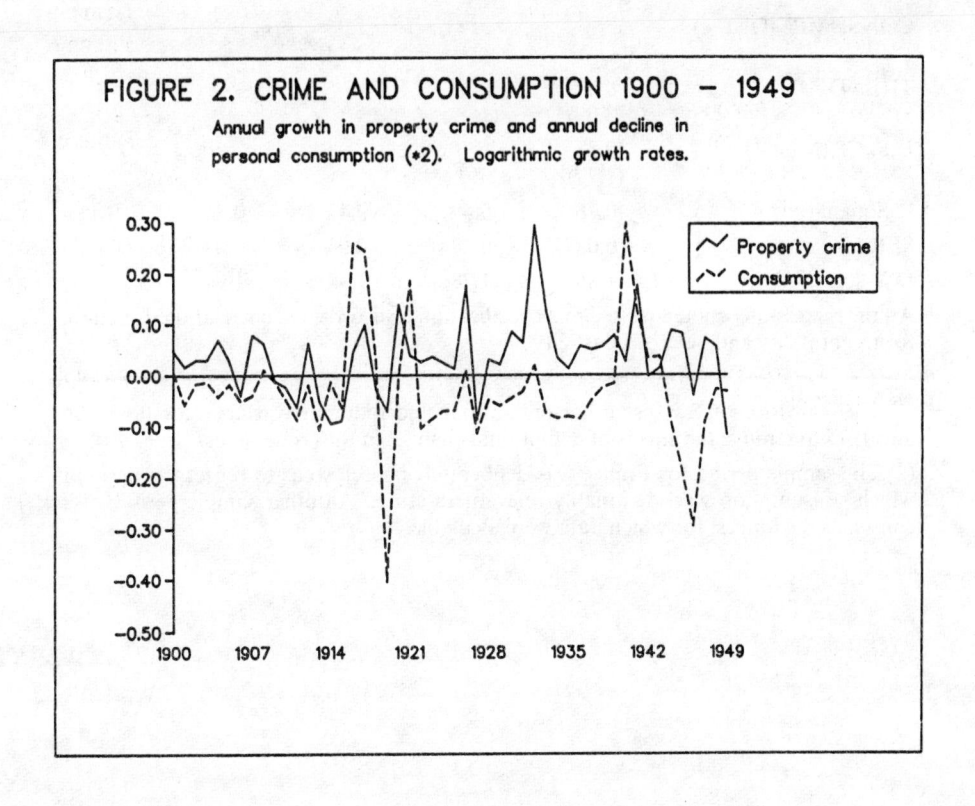

FIGURE 2. CRIME AND CONSUMPTION 1900 – 1949

Annual growth in property crime and annual decline in personal consumption (∗2). Logarithmic growth rates.

TRENDS IN CRIME AND THEIR INTERPRETATION

Table 4

Crime and consumption: international comparisons.

Regressions using crime in different countries as dependent variable. Estimated coefficients and (in brackets) t-ratios are quoted.

Country Sample period:	U.S. 1962-86	France 1975-86(2)	Germany 1965-85	Japan 1961-85	Sweden (1) 1960-81
INTERCEPT	0.25 (2.85)	1.41 (2.12)	0.01 (0.94)	0.04 (3.56)	0.00 (0.05)
CONSUMPTION	−1.28 (2.86)	−3.98 (2.23)		−0.57 (3.43)	
CONSUMPTION(−1)			−0.77 (2.18)		1.26 (2.01)
CONSUMPTION(−2)	1.77 (4.25)		1.75 (3.53)		
CONSUMPTION(−3)			−1.26 (2.50)		
CONSUMPTION(−4)			1.05 (2.44)		
TREND	−0.07 (3.09)	0.37 (1.97)			
U.S. CRIME(−1)	0.23 (1.77)				
R-Squared	0.76	0.40	0.47	0.34	0.45
SER	0.03	0.07	0.03	0.03	0.05
DW-statistic	1.88	1.78	1.34	1.94	2.04

All the regressions quoted passed mis-specification tests for serial correlation, functional form, normality and heteroscedasticity.

---

(1) The regression on Swedish crime data also included dummy variables for 1965, 1968 and 1975 to remove the effects of definitional changes in the crime series.

(2) The sample period for France was deliberately chosen so as to reflect the period in which consumption was identifiably relevant to crime. All other sample periods were chosen as the longest for which data were available.

THE RESULTS AND THEIR INTERPRETATION

The United States.

Data for real personal consumption and recorded property crime for the 1960-86 period were examined (see figure 3):

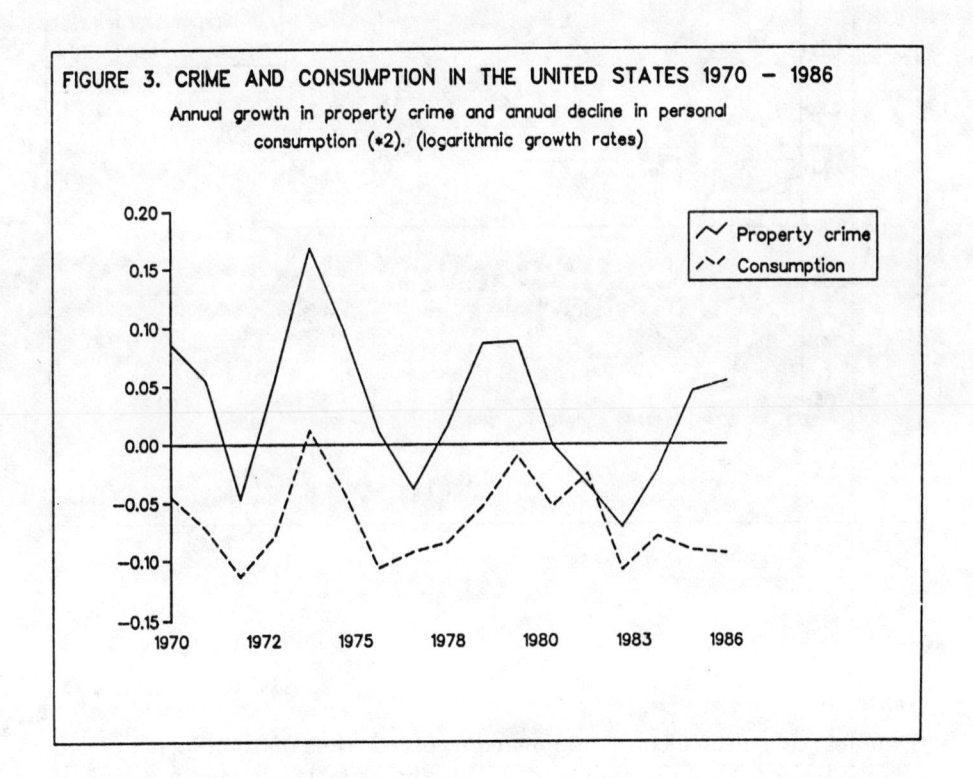

FIGURE 3. CRIME AND CONSUMPTION IN THE UNITED STATES 1970 – 1986
Annual growth in property crime and annual decline in personal consumption (*2). (logarithmic growth rates)

A strong relationship similar to that for England and Wales is evident in the data. A simple regression model was established (see table 16). The relation between consumption growth and growth in property crime is similar to that found in England and Wales except that in the United States case there is more weight on the positive effect on crime growth of previous consumption growth.

France.

Data for a real personal consumption and recorded crime for the 1959-1986 period were examined. A strong relationship as hypothesized is evident for the period since the early 1970's, but the earlier period shows little evidence of a relation. (see figure 4).

TRENDS IN CRIME AND THEIR INTERPRETATION

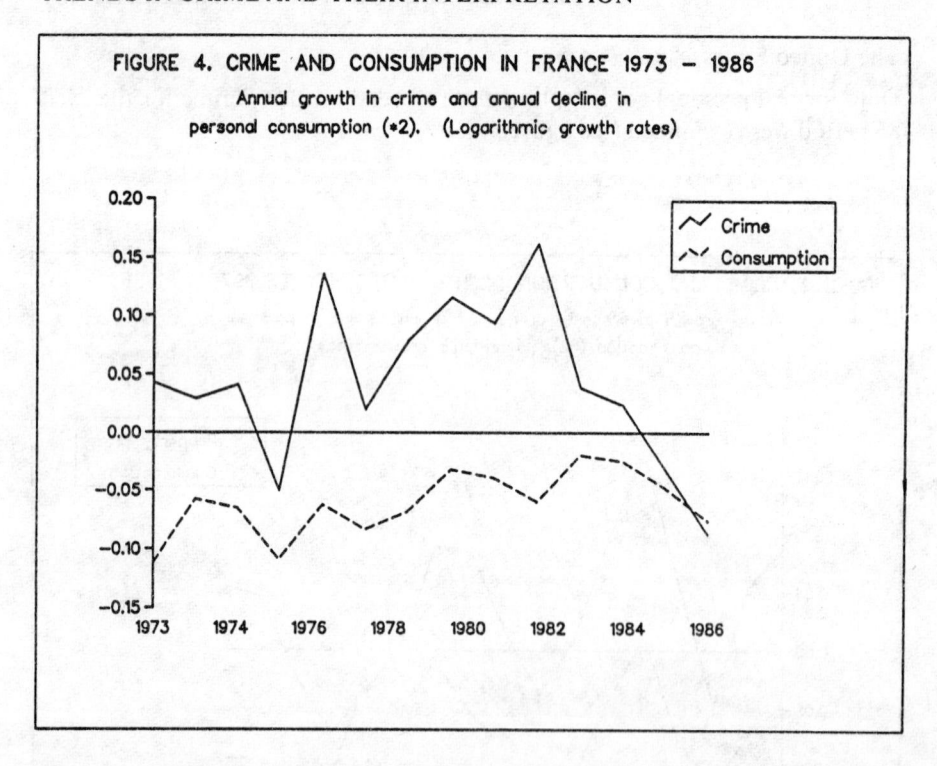

FIGURE 4. CRIME AND CONSUMPTION IN FRANCE 1973 – 1986
Annual growth in crime and annual decline in personal consumption (*2). (Logarithmic growth rates)

Germany.

Data for real personal consumption and recorded crime for the 1965-85 period were examined. West Germany is distinctive in the relatively steady growth of crime during the period (while consumption growth fluctuated markedly). Visual inspection of the series displays no obvious connection between consumption growth and crime. However this turns out to mask a strong and complex relationship displayed in the regression model in table 4. Consumption growth appears to explain much of the fluctuation in growth of recorded crime in West Germany, but the relation takes a rather unusual form and is not easy to interpret.

Japan.

Data for real personal consumption and recorded crime for the 1960-85 period were examined. Japan is an intriguing case in that crime growth has been low or negative for much of the post-war period, while consumption growth has been very high. A relationship between crime and consumption growth is apparent, particularly towards the end of the period. (see figure 5).

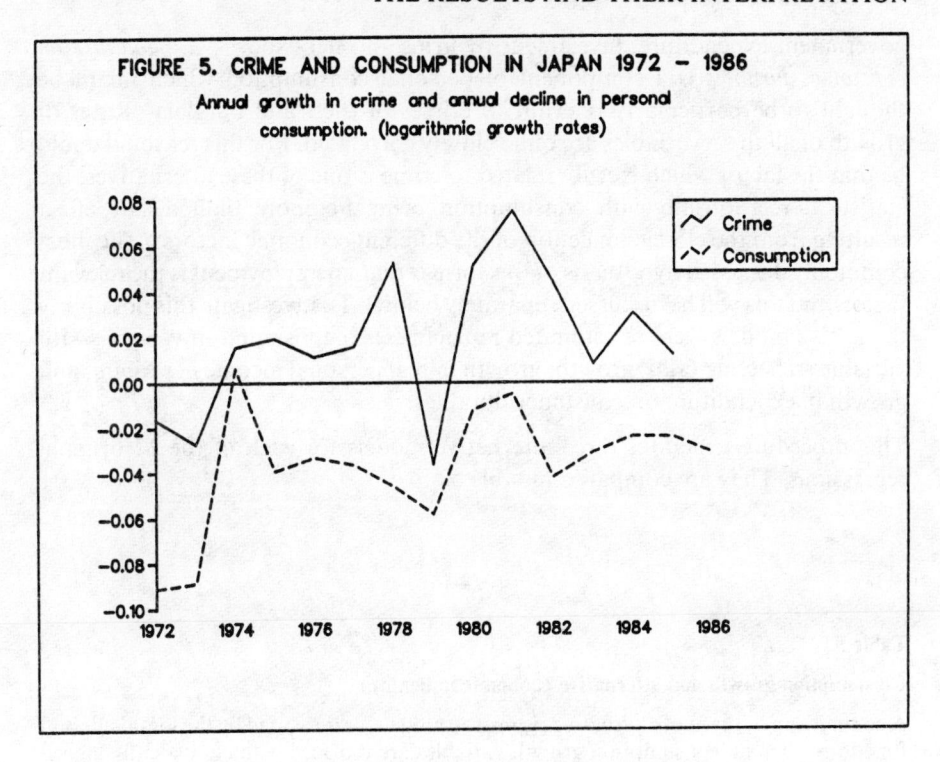

THE RESULTS AND THEIR INTERPRETATION

FIGURE 5. CRIME AND CONSUMPTION IN JAPAN 1972 – 1986
Annual growth in crime and annual decline in personal consumption. (logarithmic growth rates)

Sweden:

Data for real personal consumption and theft for the 1960-81 period were examined. No relationship was apparent on inspection of the two series, but regression analysis demonstrated a positive association between current growth in theft and past growth in consumption (see table 4).

This international comparison demonstrates that the strong inverse relationship between consumption and property crime growth rates is common in industrialised countries, but not universal. A similar pattern was found in England and Wales, the United States, and Japan and France during the last ten or fifteen years. Rather different patterns obtain in West Germay and Sweden, although in every case some relationship between consumption and crime is evident.

Consumption and other economic variables

The consumption variable used here is the annual growth of real personal consumption *per capita*. This represents the increase in household expenditure (discounting the effects of inflation) per head of population.

Personal consumption is closely related to other economic variables. *Personal income* is consumption plus savings. Personal consumption represents rather more than half of *gross domestic product*—the other components being

TRENDS IN CRIME AND THEIR INTERPRETATION

government expenditure, investment by firms and net exports. *Expenditure on consumer durables* is a component of personal consumption which might be thought to be particularly relevant to crimes of theft and burglary. Rates of growth of all these variables are quite closely correlated. For this reason it could be that the factor which is truly related to crime is one of these alternatives, the statistical relationship with consumption being no more than a side effect resulting from the close connection of the different economic factors. (The most commonly discussed hypothesis of this form is that unemployment is the relevant factor, and this will be discussed separately below). To investigate this possibility the twelve models were re-estimated replacing each consumption variable with variables reflecting GDP growth, growth in real personal income *per capita*, and growth in expenditure on consumer durables.

This procedure generates three alternative models for each of the 12 original regressions. They are compared in table 5.

Table 5
Consumption growth and alternative economic indicators

A comparison of the fit of alternative regression models, as measured by the log-likelihood functions when all consumption growth variables are replaced with equivalently lagged alternatives.

	Per capita Consumption	Expenditure on consumer durables	Per capita income	Gross Domestic Product
Residential burglary	71	66	67	62
Non-residential burglary	65	55	53	46
Theft from the person	42	40	41	39
Shop theft	75	70	68	62
Theft of vehicle	56	51	40	42
Theft from vehicle	69	65	68	61
Other theft	84	76	69	70
Robbery	52	43	44	42
Violence against the person	107	98	94	93
Sexual offences	81	76	75	79
Criminal damage	69	65	63	62
Fraud	58	57	57	55

The results are clear. None of the 36 alternative regression models can be preferred to the 12 original regressions.

Long run and short run implications

The results of the regression model relating consumption and crime are illustrated in table 6.

THE RESULTS AND THEIR INTERPRETATION

Table 6

Consumption and crime

Estimated coefficient on personal consumption variables in final models (derived from tables A.1 to A.12 in Appendix A).

	Current consumption growth	Consumption growth lagged: 1 year	2 years	3 years	4 years
Crimes undertaken for gain					
Residential burglary	−1·4		+1·3		
Non-residential burglary	−2·3		+3·1		
Theft from the person			+2·0		
Theft from a shop	−3·1		−1·8		
Theft of vehicle	−3·2	+4·2			
Theft from vehicle	−1·1			+1·7	+0·9
Other theft	−1·8	+1·9			+0·8
Robbery	−3·0			+2·3	
Fraud		−1·2			
Other crimes against property					
Criminal damage	−3·1			−1·8	
Crimes against persons					
Violence against the person		+1·2		+0·9	
Sexual offences	+1·3		+0·9		

The points which stand out are:

1. Crimes undertaken for gain tend to show an inverse relation with current consumption growth, and a positive relation with past consumption growth.

2. 'Personal' crimes undertaken in the presence of the victim, tend to show a positive relation with current and past consumption growth.

This evidence is broadly consistent with other findings reported in the literature. As long ago as 1867 Von Mayr reported a positive association between the price of rye and property crime in Bavaria. (The price of rye was probably a good inverse indicator of real income and consumption.) For crimes against the person Von Mayr reports a more complex relationship (quoted in Mannheim, 1965). Bonger (1916) argues that theft tends to increase in times of economic depression while (violent) 'crimes of vengeance' and probably sexual crimes tend to increase in periods of prosperity. Although he questions the implied inevitability, Bonger refers to the frequent recognition that economic crimes (such as theft) occur in periods of depression, while crimes against the person occur in periods of prosperity. In a statistical study of crime in England and Wales, Thomas (1925) found some inverse correlation over time between economic prosperity and property crime, and some indication of a positive correlation with offences against the person. Radzinowicz (1971) states that enquiries have shown that

> .. during periods of prosperity and depression, larceny and assaults move in converse directions. Crimes against the person (such as assault and battery)

tend to go up during a period of prosperity and often decrease during a depression. A similar trend has been observed with respect to sexual offences.

Curiously enough, this idea has been somewhat eclipsed in more recent work on crime trends and the economy, perhaps because many of the more recent studies have tended to concentrate on unemployment. For example Box (1987) surveys the recent literature on recessions and crime primarily in terms of measures in unemployment and income inequality, and their hypothesized (positive) effect on crime. Such studies are clearly important, but the evidence presented here suggests that an older theoretical tradition also has much to offer.

The nature of the effects identified in these models requires some careful discussion. First, the analysis conducted here is designed to analyse the effect of different factors on the *growth rate* of crime. It does not therefore bear directly on explanations of the level of crime. Second, it is important to distinguish between short run and long run effects. Formally, the short run effect of consumption growth on the growth of a particular sort of crime will be represented by the coefficient on the current value of consumption growth in the regression. The long run effect will be represented by the sum of all the coefficients on current and lagged values of the coefficients; in the model, this assesses the impact of long run economic growth rates (as indicated by consumption growth) on the long run growth of crime. One of the most common weaknesses in the time series analyses of the relation between crime and the economy which have been conducted is a tendency to conflate these different types of causal relation into hypotheses such as 'unemployment causes crime' or 'poverty causes crime' which slide over the complex dynamic relations between crime and the behaviour of the economy.

Property crime tends to rise more slowly at times when consumption growth is speeding up. The initial negative effect on property crime of consumption growth appears to be followed a year or two later by an inverse, positive effect. The evidence for this lies in the positive estimated coefficients on lagged consumption growth in most of the regression equations for property crime. This is illustrated in table 18. A similar pattern is observable in the United States (see table 16).

The initial effect on property crime of a change in the level of consumption growth is therefore followed a year or two later by a 'bounce-back' in the opposite direction. The impact is akin to a push on a pendulum—initially it swings to the right, but in the long run its average position does not deviate. The same is true for consumption and property crime. This is broadly clear from the estimated models (although theft from the person and criminal damage appear to be something of exceptions).

A more direct way of examining the issue is to see whether there is any relation between consumption growth and property crime growth over five year periods, rather than by looking at annual growth rates. Data for the five year growth rate of property crime for the period 1901—1980 were examined. The correlation coefficient between growth in consumption and growth in property crime for the

THE RESULTS AND THEIR INTERPRETATION

16 five-year periods was exactly 0·00, strongly suggesting that there is little or no long run relation between the rate of consumption growth and growth in property crime.

Consumption and recording practice

One possible explanation for the relationship between consumption and recorded crime is that consumption affects the propensity for crime to be recorded rather than crime itself. If this is so it could either be because of an effect on reporting, or because of an effect on police practice in recording crime reported to them. It is difficult to identify any reason why the latter effect might occur: police strength, which probably does affect recording practice was separately assessed in the analysis.

The former possibility has more immediate plausibility. It might be argued that consumption growth affects reporting practice as follows. Victims of property crime have to decide whether or not they regard the incident as sufficiently serious to justify the time and trouble to report a crime to the police. People are likely to 'cost' their time partly in relation to their spending power—a millionaire will normally require a larger financial incentive than a pauper to give up an hour of time. This suggests that increased spending power and consumption could result in less willingness to spend the time necessary to report a crime. As a result consumption growth reduces reporting and generates a lower level of recorded crime.

The argument is not without its difficulties. Consumption growth involves the purchase of items such as telephones and means of transport which reduce the time taken to report crime. Increased purchases of insurance may also increase reporting. Moreover as consumption rises, so may the average value of any given theft, and hence the incentive to report theft in the hope that the property will be recovered. From a theoretical standpoint, consumption growth may have a positive as well as negative effect on reporting.

The outcome was investigated empirically by examining the relation of consumption growth to the number of recorded thefts and burglaries. If, as hypothesized, consumption growth tends to reduce the likelihood that a loss of a low value will be reported, then consumption growth should tend to depress the proportion of reported thefts with nil losses. Data were examined for the period 1974-87 for residential and non-residential burglary, theft from the person, theft from the vehicle and all theft. Simple regression models were established examining the relation of growth in the proportion of recorded offences without loss to consumption growth. For none of the offences mentioned did evidence emerge that the proportion of reported offences with nil losses was associated with personal consumption. This analysis therefore offers no support for the hypothesis that consumption growth leads to a lower level of reporting, and therefore recording.

TRENDS IN CRIME AND THEIR INTERPRETATION

These considerations can be backed up by more direct evidence. There is consistent evidence that the offence of vehicle theft is more often reported and recorded than any other type of offence. According to the 1987 British Crime Survey 86 per cent. of such offences were recorded by the police (Mayhew, Elliott and Dowds, 1989). However the results from this study also show that theft of vehicles displays one of the strongest links with consumption of any type of crime. If the effect were attributable to recording, it would be expected that, of all types of property crime, theft of vehicles would display the *weakest* relation with consumption growth. This is strongly confirming evidence that the effect of consumption on recorded crime is one which relates to actual levels of crime, rather than recording or reporting practice. There is an important corollary. Given that much of the variation in recorded property crime growth is attributable to consumption growth, and this reflects an actual rather than a reporting or recording effect, much of the year on year variation in recorded property crime growth must reflect changes in actual crime, rather than fluctuations in recording and reporting.

An interpretation of the relation between crime and consumption

Three fields of theoretical literature have been drawn on as a foundation for an interpretation of the relation between crime and consumption. They will first be described.

First, under the modern economic theories of consumption developed by Friedman (1957), Ando and Modigliani (1963) and others, it is argued that current levels of personal consumption are primarily determined by the expected lifetime stream of income and wealth, rather than by current income. The idea behind this is that people do not have to match current consumption to current income. In any one year, they can choose to consume less than they earn and save the rest, or borrow in order to consume more than they earn. However over a lifetime, or in the long term, people are constrained to limit their spending to that permitted by their lifetime wealth and income. With this constraint in mind, people will limit their current consumption according to their expected income in the long term. A person expecting a legacy may happily run up debts, while someone approaching retirement without a pension may save heavily.

It follows that current consumption tends to reflect long term income expectations, and a change in consumption reflects a change in those long term expectations. In a real sense, therefore a change in consumption reflects a much more fundamental reassessment of economic circumstances than does a change in disposable income, which might, for example, reflect adverse circumstances which are known to be temporary.

Second, under the economic theory of crime developed by Becker (1974), Ehrlich (1974) and others, it is argued that individuals allocate their time to a mix of legitimate and illegitimate activities in order to maximise their wealth. The amount of time devoted to illegitimate activities depends partly on the benefits to be obtained from such activity, partly on the associated risks, and partly on the competing rewards obtainable from devoting time to legitimate work. One very plausible implication of this theory is that an increase in the returns from illegitimate activity will increase the amount of such activity. The theory also implies that an increase in returns from legitimate activity will increase the time devoted to it, and hence reduce the amount of time given over to illegitimate activity.

This theory has been subject to much criticism: some have argued that work creates opportunities for crime, as well as occupying the time of persons who might otherwise be offending; Heineke (1978) has argued that legitimate work may displace leisure rather than illegitimate activity. However the main difficulty in applying this theory has always been that of separately identifying potential legal and illegal returns. Potential illegal returns from thefts and burglaries will usually depend on the quantity of goods available, most of which will have been purchased out of the returns from legal activity. Potential legal and illegal returns are therefore closely correlated, but the economic theory of crime predicts that they will have opposite effects. For these reasons there is considerable ambiguity in the interpretations offered in the empirical literature. As Orsagh and Witte (1981) point out, *per capita* income has been used in one set of studies as an index of legitimate income, and in another set as an indicator of *illegitimate* income. One attempt to get round this difficulty has been the study by Cantor and Land (1985) in which they argue on the basis of a time series study of post-war United States data that unemployment has a contemporaneous negative effect on the opportunities for crime, and perhaps a lagged motivational effect on property crime.

Orsagh and Witte survey the empirical research studies on the relation between economic status and crime and conclude that these 'provide exceedingly thin support for an income-crime relation'. The strength of evidence emerging from this study requires a revision of this view, but Orsagh and Witte's methodological strictures remain critical. The reality is that aggregate measures of economic well-being, such as the measure of personal consumption used in this study, are indicators of returns from *both* legal *and* illegal activity, and any adequate economic theory of crime needs to address this point.

Third, the 'routine activity' theory of crime provides a basis for the analysis of other economic effects on crime. Cohen and Felson (1979) argue that crimes which involve 'someone definitely and intentionally taking or damaging the person or property of another' depend on the convergence in space and time of (1) motivated offenders (2) suitable targets and (3) the absence of capable guardians against a violation. These convergences in turn depend upon the pattern of 'routine activities' in a community. They argue that the postwar period has been characterised by a shift in routine activities away from the home into activities outside the home, particularly outside work. Since being outside the home may remove a 'capable guardian' from home-based property, and as

TRENDS IN CRIME AND THEIR INTERPRETATION

victimisation rates for many types of crime are higher outside the home, (where the three conditions of crime noted above are more often satisfied), the quantity of crime has gradually risen because of this shift in routine activities.

A view of the economic determinants of certain routine activities can usefully be added to Cohen's and Felson's analysis. Persons with more money can afford the transport to take them out of the home, the costs of entertainment and refreshment in the places they visit, and perhaps the childcare and other domestic help that frees them from the need to be at home.

According to the Family Expenditure Survey, households with large incomes tend to spend a higher proportion of that larger income on leisure, and spend more in absolute terms on alcoholic drink consumed away from home, on cinema admissions, and other entertainment. (Social Trends, 18, 1988, table 10.18) According to the General Household Survey (1985), persons towards the middle of the socio-economic spectrum are more likely to go out for a meal or drink, or attend the cinema, or go on some other outing than were persons in unskilled manual occupations. (They were however, not more likely to attend football matches). While the inference from cross-section to time series is not without peril, these results strongly suggest that consumption growth results in more time being spent outside the home.

Evidence can be amassed from many sources that more time spent outside the home is strongly associated with higher levels of victimisation. Cohen and Felson (1979) quote the United States evidence in support of this. In the British Crime Survey, Hough and Mayhew (1983) demonstrate that those who spend several evenings a week out are more likely to be victims of assault. In an international victimisation survey covering 14 countries, Van Dijk, Mayhew and Killias (1990) report that for *all* types of crime one of the key determinants of victimisation rates is the frequency of going out in the evening. Moreover this relationship held for each of the 14 countries surveyed.

These findings are consistent with Cohen and Felson's 'routine activity' theory of crime. The perspective implies a positive influence of levels of income and consumption on crime.

Drawing together these threads, consumption growth might have three sorts of effect on crime:

(i) It increases both the number and value of goods available for theft. In a crime such as cycle theft increased consumption may increase the number of targets and hence opportunities for crime. Many commentators, following Wilkins (1974) have argued that crime increases as the number of opportunities for crime increase. In a crime such as burglary, increased consumption tends to increase the returns for each crime. According to the economic theory of crime this will tend to increase the incentive to commit crime, and hence the amount of crime. The increase in opportunities and returns may collectively be described as the *opportunity effect*.

THE RESULTS AND THEIR INTERPRETATION

(ii) Consumption growth indicates increased expectations of lifetime income. These increased expectations of (generally) lawful income will reduce the temptation of illegitimate activity. This may be described as the *motivation effect*.

(iii) Consumption growth increases the amount of time spent outside the home and hence the opportunities for crime. This may be termed the *routine activity effect*.

Of these three explanations, the first and third imply a positive relation between consumption and crime, while the second implies an inverse association. Both the empirical evidence, and the explanations listed above bear differently on property crime and personal crime. They will consequently be discussed separately.

Property crime

Growth in property crime, it will be recalled, has an inverse relation to consumption growth in the short run, but in the long run displays no relation. The 'motivation effect' is the only explanation cited which implies an inverse relation. This suggests that the motivation effect of consumption on property crime is dominant in the short run, but in the long run it is balanced out by the opportunity and routine activity effects, both of which involve a positive relation of consumption to property crime.

Two reasons may be advanced for why the motivation effect is dominant in the short run. First, the statistical relationship which we are concerned to explain is an *aggregate* relationship between consumption and property crime. The motivation effect occurs through the consumption of potential *offenders*. The opportunity effect, and to a great extent the routine activity effect occur through the consumption of potential *victims*. When a change in the aggregate level of consumption occurs, it may be reflected differently in the population of potential victims than in the population of potential offenders. Although there are variations in the risk of victimisation, potential victims of recorded crime are a widely spread group. Potential offenders, in the slightly special sense of those who are predominantly responsible for recorded crime, are a tightly clustered group. All the evidence suggests that a particular sub-group of young men are responsible for a substantial proportion of all recorded crime. Their position in the labour market will certainly be distinctive, from which it follows that national changes in consumption may be reflected in a particular manner in this group.

Studies of the labour market in recent years, such as that by Doeringer and Piore (1985) have tended to emphasise its 'divided' or 'segmented' quality. Doeringer and Piore argued that the 'primary' labour market consists of secure, full-time often unionised employment, whereas the secondary labour market consists of insecure, temporary or part-time workers. From a somewhat different perspective economists such as Lindbeck and Snower (1986) have argued that 'insiders' in the labour market have power over wage negotiating machinery which they use to the disadvantage of 'outsiders' whose position in the labour market is more tenuous. Most of these theories have one thing in common. They imply that during recessions, the burden of the recession, including unemployment and short-time working falls disproportionately on certain marginal groups. Conversely during economic upturns, the same marginal groups benefit disproportionately.

This idea is also not new. The introduction to the 1908 Criminal Statistics (Home Office, 1910) suggest that one group of offenders are those on the

> ... fringe of industry, who in prosperous times are able to earn a living honestly, but who, in periods of trade depression and unemployment, are the first to feel the pinch of poverty and distress, and at such times are easily driven to commit crime.

It is argued that since other groups of offenders are relatively constant over time the offences of this particular group of offenders 'mainly control the fluctuations in the totals of recorded crime'.

All that we know about potential offenders suggests that they will be located in these marginal groups who are particularly vulnerable to fluctuations in the national economy. Consequently, fluctuations in national levels of consumption will tend to be amplified in the level of consumption among potential offenders. The motivation effect will therefore also be amplified. Among potential victims, although consumption will not necessarily exactly match national levels of consumption, the social spread of potential victims will ensure that the pattern of consumption among this group is not too dissimilar to the national pattern. Consequently national aggregate levels of consumption may adequately represent the opportunity and routine activity effects.

It follows that in the short term, the amplified motivation effect will tend to dominate over the opportunity and routine activity effects. However the form of amplification is in essence short term—both upswings and downswings in the economy are amplified in their effect on potential offenders. In the absence of other underlying trends in the labour market, long-run rates of consumption growth among potential offenders will tend to match national levels of consumption growth. This means that in the long run, the motivation effect in an unamplified form will be balanced by the opportunity and routine activity effects.

The second reason is almost certainly interconnected. Change in the level of consumption implies change in expectations about future income. Downward changes in these expectations may generate frustration, and a type of deprivation relative to previous expectations. These circumstances may be conducive to the breakdown of social controls. By similar reasoning, Davies (1969) argues that social rebellions are most likely when 'a prolonged period of rising expectations and rising gratifications is followed by a short period of sharp reversal, during which the gap between expectations and gratifications quickly widens and becomes intolerable.' Davies argues that the frustration which then develops can become focused on the government, leading to social rebellions, and quotes historical evidence for this effect. By a closely analogous argument, it could be maintained that the social controls which inhibit crime are undermined when rising economic expectations are suddenly reversed.

The point of this argument is that it goes beyond the simple economic point that a reduction in opportunities for lawful material gain may increase the temptation of competing criminal activity undertaken for gain, and adds a sociological perspective. The weakness of the pure economic theory of crime is that there are clearly many circumstances when people do not commit crimes which would materially benefit them. The breakdown of social controls is in effect a precondition for the economic determinants of crime to have full play. However the breakdown of those social controls may also in its turn be determined partly by economic circumstances. By Davies' argument, circumstances in which expectations are frustrated will tend to undermine those controls.

The argument also has the merit of explaining why the effect is limited to the short run. A long period of economic stagnation will not generate any expectations to be frustrated, and social controls may be maintained under those conditions. The effect follows from a sudden departure from trend.

Some specific evidence about particular crimes is relevant here. Criminal damage and theft of vehicles both show a strong short run inverse association (in growth rates) with consumption. Criminal damage however, is obviously not undertaken for gain, and much vehicle theft, in the form of joy-riding, is not motivated by directly material considerations. It follows that the association cannot be explained by a decline in consumption resulting in a compensatory search for illegitimate gain. However these results could be explained by the undermining of social controls following an economic downturn.

To sum up, in the short term, the motivation effect of consumption on potential offenders tends to dominate over other effects mediated through victims. It does so for two reasons: first, fluctuations in national levels of consumption will tend to be amplified among potential offenders who are likely to be situated in disadvantaged and vulnerable sectors of the labour market; second, sharp changes in the economic expectations of offender groups may result in frustration and undermine the social controls inhibiting offending.

Personal crime

Whereas growth in property crime is negatively associated with consumption growth in the short run, personal crimes—including both violence against the person and sexual offences— are positively associated with consumption both in the short and long run. Two reasons can be advanced to explain this pattern.

First, of the three potential explanations of a relation between crime and consumption, the first and second are irrelevant to personal crime, since they refer to the opportunities and motivation of property crime. This leaves the third 'routine activity' explanation, whereby increasing consumption leads to an increase in the amount of time spent outside the home, and increased victimisation as a result. This suggests that the only factor at work is one

TRENDS IN CRIME AND THEIR INTERPRETATION

involving a positive relation between consumption and crime. Second, the effect of routine activities on levels of victimisation appears to be particularly strong in the case of personal crime. Evidence for this finding emerges from the International Telephone Survey. Those who went out in the evening 'almost daily' were more than three times as likely both to report being the victims of assaults and threats, and being the victims of sexual incidents as those who went out less than once a month. Although frequency of going out was associated with the risk of victimisation for other crimes as well, the effect is generally weaker, with the exception of the crime of personal theft. (Van Dijk, Mayhew and Killias, 1990).

In this study, personal crimes—violence against the person, sexual offences, and theft from the person (but not robbery)—all show a positive association with consumption growth in the preceding year or two. This result may be readily interpreted as an effect of spending more time outside the home—a 'routine activity' effect. In figure 6, consumption growth is plotted against the growth of personal crime (violence against the person and sexual offences). Particularly during the last twenty years, growth in personal crime has closely tracked consumption growth.

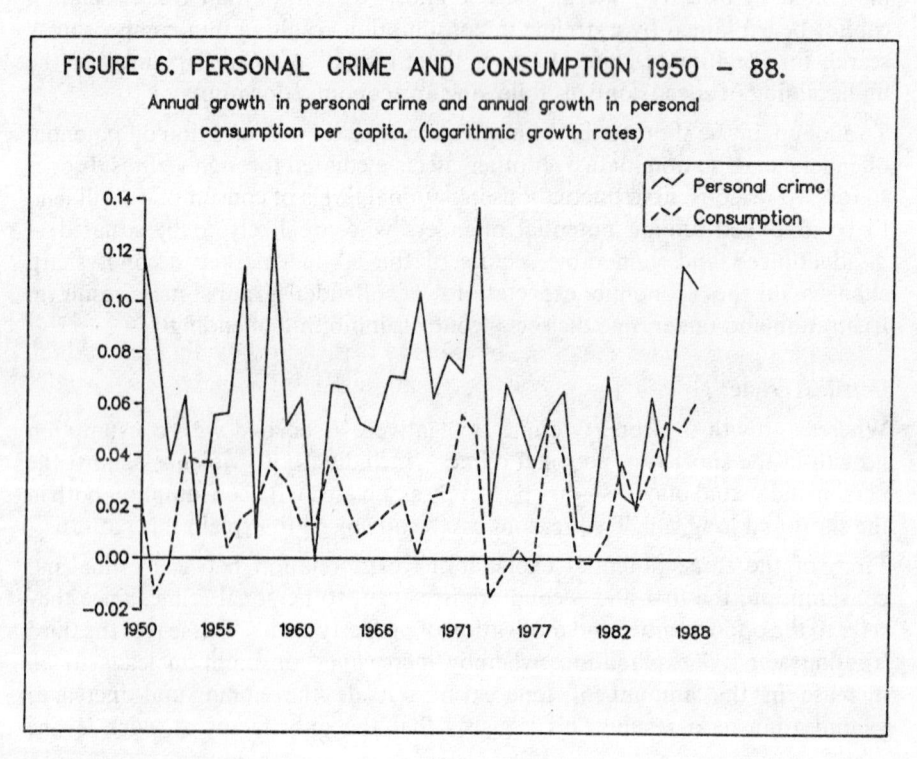

FIGURE 6. PERSONAL CRIME AND CONSUMPTION 1950 – 88.
Annual growth in personal crime and annual growth in personal consumption per capita. (logarithmic growth rates)

THE RESULTS AND THEIR INTERPRETATION

This relationship is therefore the reverse of that found between property crime and consumption growth. One simple way of presenting this result is in the form of correlation coefficients, which show the strength of statistical relationships between different factors (see table 7).

Table 7
Relationship between consumption, property and personal crime.
Correlation matrix of annual growth rates 1970-88. Property crime includes theft, burglary and robbery.

	Consumption	*Property crime*	*Personal crime*
Consumption	1.00		
Property crime	−0.81	1.00	
Personal crime	0.57	−0.60	1.00

Consumption growth is strongly inversely related to the growth of property crime, and somewhat less strongly, is positively related to the growth of personal crime. As a result, during consumption booms personal crime tends to rise faster while property crime grows more slowly or falls.

This analysis has an immediate application to recent trends in rates of recorded crime. Between 1986 and 1988 recorded property crime fell by a few per cent while offences of violence against the person and sexual offences continued to rise at around 10 per cent each year. Some of these increases may reflect reporting and recording practice rather than actual rises (Davidoff and Dowds, 1989), but the imbalance has naturally led to some anxiety that inadequate attention is being given to the prevention of personal crime.

An explanation for this pattern is now apparent. It is entirely typical of this phase in the business cycle in which consumption growth reaches a peak. Given that property and personal crime have opposite associations with consumption growth, the good figures for property crime occur simultaneously with poor figures for personal crime. Similar phases of previous business cycles show patterns which are very similar to those of 1987-88. The last two two-year periods during which consumption growth peaked were 1971-73 and 1977-79.

—Between 1971 and 1973, consumption grew by 10 per cent in real terms; the number of recorded thefts remained constant while burglary fell by 14 per cent. Meanwhile violence against the person rose by 27 per cent and sexual offences by 9 per cent.

—Between 1977 and 1979 consumption grew by 9 per cent; theft offences fell by 5 per cent and burglary by 10 per cent. Violence against the person rose by 14 per cent and sexual offences by 2 per cent.

TRENDS IN CRIME AND THEIR INTERPRETATION

Unemployment

The theory that unemployment causes crime has a long and chequered history in criminology. Some studies on individual level data have suggested that persons are more likely to commit crimes when unemployed (Farrington *et al.*, 1986) but evidence from studies on aggregate data is equivocal (Orsagh and Witte, 1981, Tarling, 1982). During economic booms, consumption tends to rise and unemployment falls. During recessions this process goes into reverse: consumption falls and unemployment rises. Could the relationship between crime and economic conditions described here not therefore be attributed to unemployment rather than to consumption growth?

The main obstacle to this interpretation can be stated simply. As people spend more, retailers sell more of their stocks, pass orders back to manufacturers and producers who may then increase production and take on more employees. But this process takes time. This means that current consumption growth tends to be reflected in unemployment decline a year or so in the future. It has been shown that current growth in consumption is, inversely, strongly related to current growth in property crime. Growth in property crime therefore anticipates growth in unemployment. This relation cannot, for obvious reasons, be interpreted as one of unemployment causing crime.

This objection does not apply to a reinterpretation of the effects of past consumption growth on crime. However there is usually a positive association between past consumption growth and current crime growth; this would imply an inverse relationship between unemployment and crime. Although it is possible to think of reasons why such a relationship might exist—some of them have been suggested by Cantor and Land (1975), it does not bear on the main hypothesis of interest, which is that of whether the experience of unemployment tends to lead people to crime.

Unemployment showed a distinctive relation to offences of violence against the person, and this will be described below.

For the other eleven types of crime covered in this study, three unemployment variables were added to the regressors in the models—current unemployment, and unemployment one or two years previously (expressed logarithmically). This formulation should be sufficient to identify any effect of the level or growth rate of unemployment on the growth of crime. The results could not be clearer. The statistical tests showed no evidence for any unemployment effect on any of these types of crime. Individual t-tests were carried out on each of the 33 estimated coefficients as were 11 f-tests on the three regressor coefficients taken together. In each of the 44 cases, the null hypothesis that the true coefficients on the unemployment variables were zero could not rejected at the five per cent level. Moreover, even when the unemployment variables were added to the models, the vast majority of estimated consumption growth coefficients remained significantly non-zero. Of course if consumption growth is removed from the picture, by dropping all consumption variables from the models, a statistical

THE RESULTS AND THEIR INTERPRETATION

relationship between crime and unemployment can sometimes be identified. But the relationship is weak, and there can be no justification for removing consumption from the picture given the strong theoretical reasons, described above, for believing consumption might be related to crime.

Both the power, and limitations of this result deserve some further dissusion. First this study demonstrates that in Britain, fluctuations in all types of crime with the exception of crimes of violence against the person are not to any discernible extent associated with aggregate levels of unemployment. Good reasons can be advanced for trusting the results of this study rather than the myriad of sometimes contrasting results in the literature. Aggregate studies of crime and unemployment are either cross-sectional studies of different places at the same time, or time series of the same place at different times. Cross-sectional studies face the considerable difficulty that unemployment in a particular place is very difficult to disentangle from a host of other factors reflecting social disadvantage which are strongly associated with unemployment, and potentially also with crime. Over time, unemployment rises and falls quite rapidly and substantially without large changes in other factors such as housing conditions, family, educational cultural or demographic circumstances. Time series are therefore a much more effective test-bed for the hypothesis that unemployment causes crime. Among time series studies, none of those carried out either in the United States or in Britain have separately assessed the relevance of consumption growth, which appears to be the most important single variable determining fluctuations in the annual growth of crime in this country and, possibly, the United States. The effect of that omission is that the statistical relationships reported between crime and unemployment in such time series studies are unreliable; in effect they are reporting statistical relationships between crime and unemployment which are no more than a side-effect of the stronger underlying relationship between crime and consumption. On these grounds the negative result of this study must be counted as more reliable.

The qualification to this result is that it refers to aggregate data. Even if trends in national levels of unemployment are unrelated to trends in national levels of crime, it does not follow that unemployment cannot cause crime. For a potential or actual offender, the experience of unemployment might precipitate offending or an increase in the rate of offending, and there is some direct evidence that persons who are unemployed are more likely to become involved in crime (Farrington et al., 1986). An increase in the rate of unemployment in the social group which is at risk of becoming involved in crime could therefore increase the rate of offending by this sub-group, even though, for most people, no such causal relation exists. Moreover, as potential and actual offenders are unlikely to have a labour market position representative of the population as a whole, fluctuations in the rate of unemployment among this group may take a very different pattern from fluctuations in the national rate of unemployment. It follows that fluctuations in aggregate unemployment could be independent of fluctuations in crime, even though unemployment is causing crime.

There are arguments both for and against this hypothesis. For this hypothesis, the explanation previously advanced to explain the cyclical effects of consumption on crime rests on the assumption that the business cycle has a different (greater) impact on actual and potential offenders than on society as a whole. It would be consistent with this explanation for the group to also experience a pattern of unemployment which differs from that affecting the whole labour market. Indeed, during recessions, one explanation for a sharply lower level of consumption growth in this group could well be unemployment itself.

Against the hypothesis, we may note the strength of the empirical finding that fluctuations in the level of unemployment appear to add nothing to the explanation of different types of crime (with the exception of violence against the person) once consumption growth is taken into account. If unemployment is a major cause of crime, then we would expect changes in the level of unemployment among potential or actual offenders to have *some* association with total unemployment, even if there are some major differences. For this reason we would expect aggregate unemployment to add something rather than nothing to the explanation of crime. Further research is necessary to clarify this point.

Crime and demographic change

The amount of crime depends not only on the size of the population but also on its age-structure. One reason for this is that involvement in crime is more common among young males than among women or older men. The age and sex composition of those found guilty and cautioned of notifiable crimes bears this out. In 1987, of those found guilty or cautioned 85 percent were men, and 42 percent were men under 21.

An increase in the number of young males can therefore have a substantial impact on the overall crime rate. For example if the age-composition of those found guilty and cautioned accurately reflects age-specific crime rates, we would expect a 10 percent increase in the number of males aged 10 to 20 to be associated with an increase in recorded crime of four percent.

Assessing the relation of demographic trends to those in crime is subject to a particular difficulty. Change in the numbers of persons in particular age and sex groups tend to go in one direction for several years before reversing itself; change in the number in any one year is therefore closely correlated with change in the previous year. This means that estimation of the effects of demographic change on recorded crime tends to be somewhat unreliable, because the estimation procedure cannot unambiguously pick out the effect of one year's change from the next. This difficulty means that the results from this part of the study must be treated with some caution.

THE RESULTS AND THEIR INTERPRETATION

To assess the overall impact of demographic change on crime, the models were re-estimated replacing all the demographic variables with a variable reflecting growth in the number of males aged 10-29. The results are given in table 8.

Table 8
Crime and demographic change

Percentage growth in crime associated with a one per cent growth in the number of males aged 10-29.

	Estimated Coefficient	*Standard Error*
Residential burglary	1·0	0·7
Non-residential burglary	0·4	1·7
Theft from person	1·8	1·5
Shop theft	4·7	0·9
Theft of vehicle	1·5	1·7
Theft from vehicle	1·2	1·6
Other theft	0·2	0·8
Robbery	0·2	2·0
Violence against person	0·8	0·8
Sexual offences	−0·8	0·9
Criminal damage	6·1	1·8
Fraud	4·3	1·1

The results quoted in this table can be interpreted alongside the individual regression results quoted in Appendix A, in which five-year age-bands were used to reflect demographic effects.

First, nearly all the estimated coefficients are positive. This implies that growth in the numbers of young men does increase the amount of recorded crime. However, for some types of crime at least, the size of the demographic effect is surprisingly large. If all the crime of a particular type were carried out by males aged 10-29, then we would expect that the 'arithmetic' effect of one per cent increase in the numbers in this group would be a one per cent increase in the amount of crime. In fact, for shop theft, criminal damage and fraud a one per cent increase in the male population aged 10-29 is associated with much more than a one per cent increase in the relevant crime rates. For many other sorts of crime, such as theft from the person and vehicle crime, there is weaker evidence for the same sort of 'excess' effect. The evidence suggests that demographic change may have effects on rates of recorded crime over and above the purely arithmetic effects we expect.

These results are consistent with a hypothesis advanced by Easterlin (1968). He has argued that, given a social opportunity structure and means of social control which have only a limited flexibility—a bounded capacity to respond effectively to sudden changes in the size of the population seeking opportunities and requiring social control—persons in large age cohorts will face relatively fewer opportunities for social advancement, and relatively fewer social controls, than persons in small age cohorts. Maxim (1986) offers some evidence that this effect may be identifiable in England and Wales. The implication is that persons in large age cohorts are more likely to become involved in crime than persons in small age cohorts. As a result, an increase in the number of young men will not only increase crime rates because there are more persons in the crime-prone age groups, but also because the crime rate for persons in those age groups will rise.

Interaction between crimes of different types

The different categories of crime discussed here are closely related to each other in their causes and effects. The prevalence of one type of crime can influence the prevalence of another. These interactions were explored within the framework of the statistical models developed here.

Two sorts of effects are of particular interest. First, the commission of one type of crime may lead on in the same or different individuals to the commission of another sort of crime. If it is the same individual we may consider the relationship to be one of different stages in a criminal career. Petty crime requiring few skills might lead gradually to more sophisticated sorts of crime with higher returns. If different individuals are involved then the relationship implies something about the social evolution of crime: an increase in one type of crime may signify an early stage in the breakdown of social controls which is subsequently reflected in more serious types of crime. These types of relation we may describe as an 'evolutionary effect'. It implies a positive relation between the two types of crime.

Second, when one type of crime, for one reason or another, becomes more difficult or less lucrative, this crime becomes less common, but criminals may respond by devoting more of their time to an alternative sort of crime, which will become more common as a result. Conversely, when one crime becomes easier and more lucrative, it may become more common as others become less so. In line with the usual terminology, this may be termed a 'displacement effect'.

The simplest way of looking at relationships between crime growth of different types would be to plot a correlation matrix for the 12 types of crime (in growth rates) which would show us when fluctuations in one sort of crime are related to fluctuations in other sorts of crime. Such a correlation matrix was prepared, and it shows that the growth rates of all property crimes are inter-correlated, often quite strongly. The closest correlation is one between residential and non-residential burglary of 0.85. Growth in sexual offences is negatively related to growth in property crime.

These results are not surprising. Given that growth in most sorts of property crime is strongly related to consumption growth, and growth in sexual offences is inversely associated with consumption growth, different types of property crime will be correlated with each other and negatively correlated with growth in

THE RESULTS AND THEIR INTERPRETATION

sexual offences. What we do not know is whether there are any associations between crime of different types over and above associations such as these.

A more promising approach is to examine the 'residuals' from the first stage regressions. Regression models generate predictions, based on the model, of the value of crime growth for each year. These predictions ('fitted' values) will be different from the actual values. The difference between the actual and predicted value is called the residual. The size of this residual indicates how well the model 'fits'—if it were a perfect fit, all the residuals would be zero.

It follows that the actual value of crime growth in any year will be the sum of the fitted value—predicted from the model—and an unexpected element, the residual. The residual may therefore be understood as the unexpected element of crime growth.

The advantage of comparing the residuals for crime growth of different types, rather than the actual values, is that effects which can be attributed to the factors in the first stage regressions have been removed from the picture. For example the residuals for residential burglary are correlated with those for nonresidential burglary. This relation cannot now be attributed to the similar effect of consumption growth on both types of burglary, since that effect will have been reflected in the fitted values, but not the residuals. More generally, correlations between residuals suggest that 'unexpected' growth in one type of property crime tends to be associated with unexpected growth in most other sorts of property crime.

This analysis however, is also limited in its value. It is implausible to suppose that these relations reflect the fact that one property crime causes others. Instead it suggests that there are factors not included in the regression model which induce simultaneous changes in many types of crime. A host of circumstances will, plausibly, influence a range of crimes simultaneously and yet not be identifiable in a regression model such as this. It may be that there are also genuine relationships between the different types of crime—displacement and evolutionary effects, but they are almost certainly masked by the impact of common underlying factors.

One way around this difficulty is to seek clues to causal order in temporal order. In this case, the relationship of last years unexpected crime growth to crime growth of different types was therefore assessed. To achieve this the final regression models for each type of crime included as potential regressors the lagged residuals from other types of crime, and they were included where relevant. The detailed results of this analysis are included in the results for the final regressions in Appendix A. They are summarised in table 9.

It should be said at once that the conclusions drawn from this table must be extremely tentative, since the technical means of estimation is not formally correct. Given that the residuals between the equations are contemporaneously correlated, the formally correct estimation procedure will be a version of the 'Seemingly Unrelated Regression Estimator' (Zellner, 1962); in this procedure, the whole set of equations will be estimated as a whole, the residuals can be estimated iteratively, and their standard errors calculated with precision. The development of such a systematic model could be a subject for further research.

Table 9
The interaction between crime of different types

Unexpected growth in:	Associated in the following year	
	with growth in:	and decline in:
Residential burglary		Non-residential burglary, theft from vehicles, shop theft
Non-residential burglary	Robbery, violence, theft from vehicles, shop theft, criminal damage.	
Theft from the person		Residential and non-residential burglary, other theft
Shop theft	Residential burglary criminal damage	Violence
Theft of a vehicle		Robbery, theft from vehicle and person
Theft from vehicle		Theft from person criminal damage
Other theft	Non-residential burglary	
Robbery	Sexual offences	
Violence against the person		
Sexual offences		Violence
Criminal damage	Sexual offences	Residential burglary theft from vehicle, shop theft.

Where unexpected growth in one sort of crime tends to be followed after one year by growth in another sort of crime, there are two alternative causal explanations. First, it could be that some underlying process tends to affect the one sort of crime, and then, quite separately, it affects the other sort of crime. Such an explanation is always possible, but it will generally be less plausible because of the time lag between the two effects. For example, the introduction of more effective vehicle security should affect both theft from and of the vehicle simultaneously. A breakdown of social control can also be expected to affect two types of crime simultaneously.

The second explanation is that there exists a causal relation between growth in the two types of crime.

With these two hypotheses in mind, the results in table 9 can be examined. The pattern may be summarised as follows:

THE RESULTS AND THEIR INTERPRETATION

(i) There is evidence of a pattern of displacement as between different sorts of property crime. There is particularly strong evidence of displacement from residential burglary to other property crimes.

(ii) Non-residential burglary is a leading indicator of growth in a variety of other property crimes.

The first of these results is a matter of concern, given the energy currently devoted to crime prevention in general, and residential burglary in particular. One feature of the result is that it associates unexpected growth in residential burglary with decline in other crimes in the following year; it also associates unexpected decline in residential burglary with growth in other crimes during the following year. We normally think of the latter, but not the former as displacement the idea being that—say—improved physical security reduces residential burglary, and, one year later, after potential offenders have learned of the difficulties they will face in burglary, they take up other, easier crimes. The causal route from growth in residential burglary to decline in other types of property crime (after a time lag) is more problematic.

It is possible to separate these two sorts of relations, and this was carried out for residential burglary. The residual for the first stage regression for residential burglary was split into two components, whose sum is the value of the total residual, as follows: the first 'negative' part is equal to the value of the residual in any year in which it takes a negative value, zero otherwise, the second 'positive' part is equal to the value of the residual in any year in which it takes a positive value, zero otherwise. The regressions in which the residual appeared were then re-estimated, replacing the single lagged residual variable with the two 'positive' and 'negative' variables. In each of the three cases—non-residential burglary, theft from vehicles and shop theft—the 'negative' residual variable had an estimated coefficient significantly different from zero, while the 'positive' variable did not.

The interpretation is that unexpected decline in residential burglary is associated with growth in the three sorts of property crime one year later—a conventionally understood displacement effect. There is no evidence for the less intuitive inverse relation. This lends credence to the view that this is a genuine casual relation.

Given that systems estimation, as described above, will remove potential sources of error in these results, these findings as they stand are no more than exploratory. Given the importance of displacement as an issue to the assessment of crime prevention initiatives further research is clearly required in this field.

Reporting effects: insurance, telephones and tenure

A number of factors were introduced into the model on the grounds that they might be expected to relate to the reporting (and therefore recording), of crime, if not to its actual extent. These factors include the proportion of households with contents insurance, the average level of expenditure on contents insurance, the number of telephone stations. and variables which reflect the national pattern of housing tenure. As data on insurance and tenure was not available for the whole period, this analysis was conducted separately from the main excercise.

Thefts of insured goods are particularly likely to be reported because insurance policies normally require that a theft should be reported to the police before a claim is made. The availability of a telephone makes it easier to report crime to the police. Persons experiencing damage to their dwelling as a result of vandalism or burglary may be more or less likely to take it seriously enough to report the event depending on whether they are the owner of the dwelling, and if they are not, whether they have a long run interest in its maintenance.

One other issue has particular relevance to these factors. Insurance, telephones and tenure all show fairly steady long run trends. *Rates of change* in these factors will not fluctuate much over time. In the absence of substantial fluctuations, it is not possible to tell whether the factor is relevant or not. For the sake of example, suppose that the number of telephones were to grow by a steady one per cent a year, and as a result one half per cent more crimes are reported, and therefore recorded, every year. A modelling exercise such as the current one would be unable to identify such an effect, because there is no way of distinguishing the causal effect of telephone ownership from a simple trend in recorded crime. Conversely, if there were—say—a ten per cent surge in telephone ownership in one particular year, but not in others, we could look for a surge in recorded crime occuring in the same period. Such sharp fluctuations are conspicuously lacking in the data series for insurance, telephones and tenure.

Moreover there is an additional problem. All the variables dealt with here will be subject to measurement error. A small measurement error (say half of one per cent) will generate a proportionately much larger error in the calculated rate of change, particularly if that rate of change is small.

These caveats in mind, the impacts of these factors on the twelve crime types were assessed.

Telephones. Growth in the number of telephone stations was found to be negatively related to growth in the number of property crimes. This is the reverse of the expected effect—that more telephones lead to more reporting which in turn leads to more crime being recorded. However growth in the number of telephone stations is strongly related to consumption growth, and the negative effect of growth in the number of telephones is almost certainly a side-effect of this relation and can therefore be discounted. No other statistically significant relationships were identified.

Insurance. Growth in recorded residential burglary, other theft, and criminal damage were assessed in relation to the two insurance variables. The only statistically significant relation uncovered was a weak relation between the growth in the real average expenditure on contents insurance during the previous year and growth in recorded other theft and larceny.

THE RESULTS AND THEIR INTERPRETATION

Tenure. Changes in the national tenure pattern were found to be significantly related to changes in a number of types of crime. Increases in the proportion of households in owner occupation were found to be inversely related to the growth of recorded residential burglary and other theft during the following year. This is the reverse of the expected recording effect.

Violence against the person: beer consumption and unemployment

Figure 7 and table A.9 demonstrates that growth in beer consumption by volume is strongly related to growth in recorded offences of violence against the person. Growth in beer consumption is the single most important factor in explaining growth in violence against the person (in the absence of this variable the regression model has considerably less explanatory power, as indicated in a decline in the level of R-bar-squared from 0·90 to 0·55).

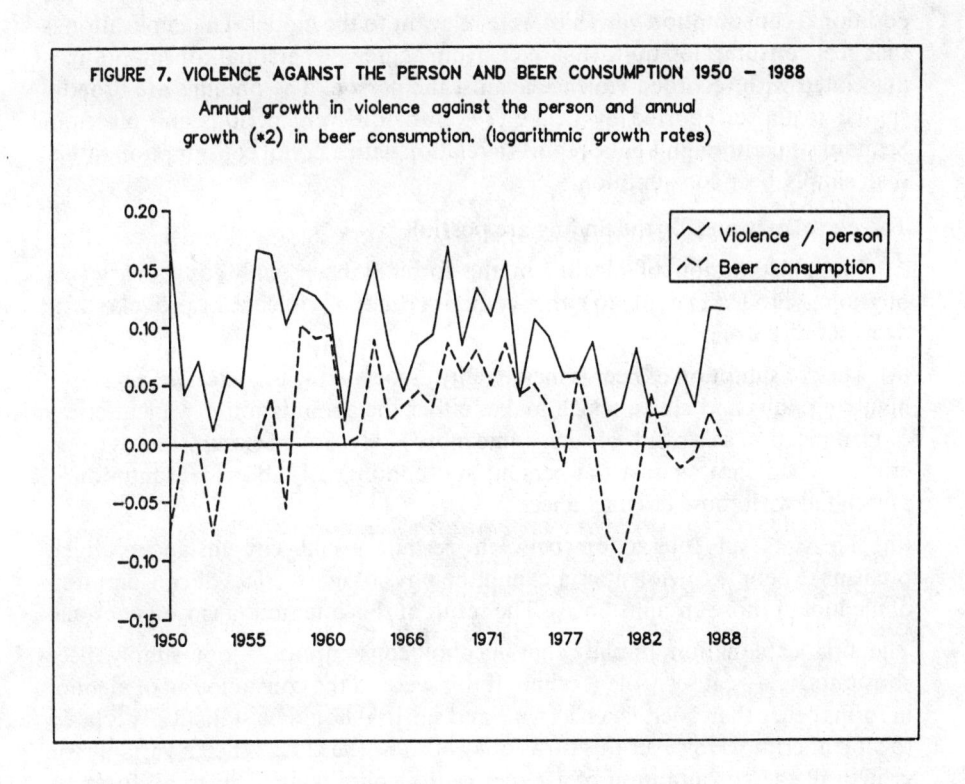

FIGURE 7. VIOLENCE AGAINST THE PERSON AND BEER CONSUMPTION 1950 – 1988
Annual growth in violence against the person and annual growth (∗2) in beer consumption. (logarithmic growth rates)

One possible explanation for this finding is that the association between beer consumption and violent crime is an incidental effect of the consumption-crime relationship, since beer consumption bears some relation to general consumption. Bonger (1916) recognising a similar relation between consumption and crimes of violence against the person argued as follows:

> It is not difficult, it seems to me, to explain why these crimes increase during periods of prosperity. Men are thrown then into contact more frequently, they live a little more for amusement, and consume (this is certainly one of the principal reasons) more alcohol than usual.

To test the hypothesis that beer consumption has an effect independently of total personal consumption, the beer consumption variable was dropped from the model and additional consumption variables (current growth and the second lag) were added in an effort to find an equally effective alternative model in which beer consumption does not occur. However there was no evidence that any of the additional consumption variables were relevant to the model. The implication is that beer consumption quite separately from aggregate personal consumption, is associated with recorded violence against the person. The findings are broadly similar to those reported by Lenke (1982) for different periods and places in Scandinavia, although Lenke reports a relation with alcohol consumption rather than simply beer consumption.

Three explanations for the finding are possible.

(i) The consumption of alcohol in the form of beer tends, as a matter of physiology, to lead people to either commit crimes of violence or provoke their own victimisation.

(ii) The consumption of beer is incidentally associated with a lifestyle, probably involving pubs and clubs, which makes either the commission of violent crime or victimisation as a result of such crime more likely. Social circumstances cause crimes of violence against the person, and contingently, beer consumption is associated with those circumstances.

(iii) There is an interaction between certain social circumstances which predispose people to violent crime, and the physiological effect of consumption of alcohol in those circumstances. The result of this interaction is violent crime.

The first explanation implies that alcohol consumption—not simply beer consumption—causes violent crime. If this were so the consumption of alcohol in forms other than beer, (such as wine and spirits) should be statistically related to violent crime. However this turns out not to be the case. When a variable for growth in the consumption of 100 per cent alcohol equivalent in all forms is added to the model, there is no evidence that it is a significant factor (t = 0.18) while the estimated coefficient on growth in beer consumption remains strongly significant (t = 5·51).

THE RESULTS AND THEIR INTERPRETATION

The evidence is clear. Growth in beer consumption, but not the consumption of other forms of alcohol is related to the growth in violence against the person. It follows that the consumption of alcohol as such cannot be regarded as a cause of violent crime.

The distinctive feature of beer-drinking, as opposed to other forms of alcohol consumption, is that much of it takes place in pubs and clubs. To assess the role of such places in the causation of violent crime, two additional variables were introduced into the model — growth in the number of off-licenses and growth in the number of on-licenses. No evidence emerged that the number of on-licenses or off-licenses is relevant to the amount of violent crime.

The most convincing explanation of these findings is that, although the consumption of alcohol itself is not a cause of violent crime, the drinking activities of particular social groups — those who drink beer — probably combined with a particular set of social circumstances, may be a factor in offences of violence against the person.

Growth in offences of violence against the person was also found to be associated with growth in unemployment during the previous year. This was the only type of crime found to be connected with unemployment, and the relation is strong. Moreover, changes in the real value of unemployment benefit during the current and previous years were also associated (negatively) with growth in offences of violence against the person. These results strongly suggest that unemployment, and the relative deprivation associated with it, are conducive to violent crime. Given the lag between the growth in unemployment and the violent crime, the relevant factor may be long term unemployment.

The power of this result is reinforced by the inclusion in the model of consumption growth (consumption growth during the previous year and the three years prior to that is positively associated with current growth in violence against the person). If unemployment does not cause violent crime, their statistical association would have to be explained as the result of some underlying factor which causes both the unemployment and violent crime. The obvious candidate is economic conditions. However the relationship between violent crime and consumption growth tends to rule this out, for it is opposite in direction to that which would be required to explain the unemployment — crime relation. During recessions, when unemployment is rising, consumption growth will be slowing. The unemployment will tend to increase the level of violent crime, while the reduction in consumption will tend to reduce its level. Recession will therefore involve two opposing impacts on the level of violent crime. In practice the positive impact of consumption growth appears dominant.

The paradoxical nature of this finding may be explained by reference to the heterogeneous nature of violent crime. It has been argued that consumption growth induces changes in lifestyle which increase the risk of personal crime; these may be the violent crimes of affluence, connected with alcohol, pubs and clubs and places of entertainment. Conversely there may be violent crimes of poverty related in part to the frustration and poverty of unemployment. Domestic violence may fall into this category.

Recent trends in offences of violence against the person have been examined by Davidoff and Dowds (1989). They suggest that some at least of the recent growth in the numbers of the offence recorded are attributable to increased reporting to the police. Given that, according to the British Crime Survey only 21 per cent. of woundings end up being recorded by the police, (Mayhew *et al,* 1989) a relatively small percentage increase in reporting could generate quite a large percentage increase in the number of recorded offences of violence against the person. This is an important point to bear in mind when explaining the rapid growth in violence against the person which has occurred during the 1980's.

The birth rate

The number of live births was included in the model in order to test the hypothesis that the birth of children has an impact on crime through the economic shock it imposes on their parents (mainly through foregone earnings). Consistent with the hypothesis, it was found that an increase in live births during the previous year is associated with increases in residential and non-residential burglary, and robbery. Increase in live births is associated with a rise in shop theft two years later (a finding whose interpretation is more dubious). The time lag is not a surprising feature, for it corresponds to a period when savings are run down and debts are run up, until lines of credit run out.

One potentially confusing feature is that the number of live births is obviously correlated with the number of males in the age-groups which have the highest level of fertility. These will be young age-groups which are prone to offending. The association between live births and crime might therefore simply reflect a relation between the number of persons in young crime-prone age groups and crime. In practice this is unlikely. First, in England and Wales, women are most likely to give birth when they are in their late twenties. Given that a male partner will commonly be a year or two older than the woman, and that there is at least a one year lag between the birth of the child and the crime-rate effect, the men with financial responsibility for the children will most likely be into their thirties, well past the peak age of offending. Second, the effects of age-structure on crime were directly and separately assessed in this study, so that the relationship of crime to live births exists over and above any demographic effects.

The weather

Good weather over the year, in the shape of absence of rain and presence of sunshine, has a positive relation with sexual offences, and a negative relation with non-residential burglary and shop theft. The pattern in these findings is not sufficient to draw any clear conclusions about the influence of weather on crime.

THE RESULTS AND THEIR INTERPRETATION

Police

There is evidence that growth in police strength is negatively related to sexual offences, theft of and from vehicles and other theft. In addition, growth in police strength appears to be positively related to the growth in violent crime. The explanation for the negative finding could be:—

(i) Increases in these crimes cause decreases in police strength.

(ii) Increases in police strength tend to reduce the recording of these crimes.

(iii) Some underlying factor causes both an increase in police strength and a simultaneous reduction in crime.

(iv) Increases in police strength have a deterrent effect on crime of these types.

The first of these explanations is implausible, being the reverse of what one might expect. Changes in the level of crime are likely to generate changes in the level of police strength as a planned response to crime, but these effects will be positive rather than negative, and almost certainly involve a time lag of a year or two.

The second explanation is also implausible. It is usually argued that growth in police strength will result in an increased amount of recording, and this recording effect may explain why growth in the level of manpower is associated with increases in violence against the person. (In the case of violent crime, the speed of police response—which may depend on police strength—may increase the chance that a reported incident will still be under way at the time police officers arrive on the scene, and therefore the likelihood that the incident will be formally recorded as a crime.)

The third explanation is possible, but there is no obvious candidate for such an underlying factor.

This leaves the hypothesis that police strength has a genuinely deterrent effect on certain types of crime. While this is not the only explanation for the results, the weakness of the main alternatives must lend credence to the deterrence hypothesis.

The clear-up rate

Growth in clear-up rates had a very limited relation to changes in the level of crime. Growth in the general clear-up rate during the previous year had a negative relation to growth in violence against the person; growth in the theft clear-up rate during the previous year had an inverse relation to growth in theft of the vehicle and other theft; growth in the clear-up rate for criminal damage two years previously had an inverse relation to criminal damage.

The denominator for the clear-up rate is the amount of recorded crime. An inverse relation with past growth in the clear-up rate (such as those which emerged in this study) might therefore simply reflect a positive relation with past growth in recorded crime. In other words the finding might reflect the fact that current growth in crime is correlated with crime growth in the previous year. To

TRENDS IN CRIME AND THEIR INTERPRETATION

assess this possibility the clear-up rate variables were replaced in the models in which they occur with the equivalent lagged dependent (crime) variable. For violence against the person, other theft and theft of the vehicle the equivalent lagged dependent variable had an estimated coefficient which was significantly non-zero, and the fit of the model, as measured by the log-likelihood function was altered only marginally. Only in the case of criminal damage was this not so. This strongly suggests that there is no real effect of changes in the clear-up rate on changes in the level of recorded crime. The single result in respect of criminal damage, with the rather odd two year lag, is of dubious significance.

Apparent cyclical effects

One of the odder features of this analysis was the apparent emergence of cyclical effects. In a number of cases, crime growth is related to its own growth three or four years previously, usually inversely. These relationships are summarised in the first column of table 10.

Table 10
Relationship of crime growth rate to previous growth rate

	Estimated coefficient on lagged dependent variable in model (lag number in brackets)	Log-likelihood of:— Standard model	Alternative model
Residential burglary	(4) −0.2	70.8	70.0
Non-residential burglary	(4) −0.3	64.6	59.6
Theft of vehicle	(4) −0.1	55.8	49.8
Theft of vehicle	(2) −0.3	as above	
Other theft	(3) −0.2	83.9	81.7
Robbery	(4) −0.2	52.3	48.6
Violence against the person	(3) −0.3	107.0	106.9
Sexual offences	(4) 0.3	80.5	75.7
Criminal damage	(3) −0.2	not applicable	

(1) **The alternative model replaces all lagged dependent variables with equivalently lagged growth of consumption per capita variables.**

The picture presented is consistent. Growth in many types of property crime is inversely related to growth in that crime three or four years previously. This is not an easy finding to interpret if accepted at face value, as implying a causal relation between crime growth three or four years previously, and current crime growth. However there is an alternative interpretation.

All these cases have one thing in common. Growth in all these types of crime is related to current growth in consumption, inversely in every case except for sexual offences. It follows that the relationship with past own growth might simply reflect a finding of a relationship with past consumption growth. Indeed such an interpretation would be consistent with results already recorded. For

THE RESULTS AND THEIR INTERPRETATION

theinterpretation would imply a positive relationship between past consumption growth and current property crime growth, and a negative relationship between past consumption growth and current growth in sexual offences. This is very much what has already been demonstrated.

To test this interpretation, the models were re-estimated by removing the lagged dependent variable and replacing them with the equivalently lagged consumption growth variable. The comparison of the 'fit' of this alternative model is offered in the final columns of table 10.

The results suggest that this interpretation is largely correct. The fit of many of the regression models, as measured by the log-likelihood, declined slightly, but this probably reflects no more than the relatively mechanical specification search which resulted in the good fit of the first model. (In effect the comparison is biassed in favour of the first chosen model.) Theft of the vehicle, and criminal damage are possible exceptions here. In the case of criminal damage, the comparison is not possible because the alternative consumption variable is already included in the model.

4 Conclusion: implications of the findings

This study has demonstrated the profound importance of economic factors in the determination of crime and has developed a framework within which trends in crime rates can be interpreted in the light of national economic circumstances.

It is not realistic to imagine that national economic policy will be determined even in part by its implication for crime. Recognition of economic influences, however, provides us with a powerful means of interpreting current trends and anticipating the immediate future. The rapid increases in personal crime, and the falls in property crime which took place during the late 1980's are both explicable at least in part in terms of the consumption boom of the period. The latest departure in the figures—the upturn in property crime towards the end of 1989—is attributable to the slowing economy of that time.

These insights substantially increase the value of statistics on recorded crime, for they allow us to see past the fluctuations resulting from economic factors to the underlying trends in crime. The danger that economically determined fluctuations in crime rates will be seen as indicating the failure or success of policy on crime and crime prevention can therefore be avoided.

The statistical models developed in the course of this research have a number of immediate applications. These models 'predict' the level of different sorts of crime on the basis of a variety of environmental factors, particularly economic and demographic factors. The prediction is based on the past relationship between these factors and crime. A sophisticated means of assessing whether any recent figures for crime represent a departure from long run trends is to examine the crime rates 'predicted' on the basis of past patterns in the data, and compare them with actual rates of recorded crime. This approach distils out of the crime figures the fluctuations which can be attributed to long run trends in crime and to factors such as economic change and demography, leaving a residual element which must be attributable to new causes, such as crime prevention schemes, changes in the recording and reporting of crime, or underlying changes in criminogenic circumstances. This procedure provides a powerful means of disentangling the host of factors which result in the observed pattern of recorded crime.

As well as interpreting current trends in crime through the use of these techniques, it is also possible to forecast some way into the future. It follows that

CONCLUSION: IMPLICATIONS OF THE FINDINGS

if we can predict future economic and demographic circumstances, we can forecast future levels of crime. The main feature of the models of crime developed here is a dependency of crime on a combination of economic and demographic factors. It follows that the models permit future levels of crime to be predicted on the basis of a combination of *predicted* future economic and demographic circumstances. The behaviour of the economy can be predicted for two or three years ahead with some reliability, while demographic circumstances can be predicted with accuracy rather further ahead. This means that it is possible to use these models to predict the level of crime a few years into the future, on the basis of the forecast behaviour of the economy and forecast demographic change. Such forecasts have a direct administrative value in that recorded crime is an important element in the demands which are placed on the police and the criminal justice system, and an element which needs to be taken into account when planning—in advance—the allocation of resources to these bodies.

Some recorded crime leads to proceedings in the courts, and some of these proceedings lead to convictions and disposals, leading in their turn to prison receptions and demands upon the probation service. For these reasons, strong statistical relationships can be demonstrated between growth rates in recorded crime and growth in the number of offenders found guilty and cautioned, prison receptions and the prison population. It follows that economic factors causing fluctuations in crime rates should also have an impact on flows through these later stages in the criminal process. This is indeed what occurs. In illustration, figures 8 and 9 plot trends in consumption against proceedings in magistrates' courts, and prison receptions. In both cases, a close relationship with the behaviour of the economy is evident.

Clearly other factors—particularly administrative and legislative factors—have a major influence on the numbers dealt with at different stages of the criminal justice system—changes in the detection of crime, the cautioning, prosecution and sentencing of offenders including policy changes and the effects of resource availability. Nevertheless, over a two to three year period, the behaviour of the economy appears to be one factor which should help to explain and forecast not only crime itself but also trends in other parts of the criminal justice system, including the demands on the courts, prisons, and probation service. Given the importance of such forecasts to planning in the allocation of resources to different parts of the criminal justice system, further research on this subject might be a priority.

The influence of economic factors on the criminal process is not limited to its effect on the quantity of recorded crime. First, fluctuations in personal consumption do not have a homogeneous influence on crime. We know that they have very different effects on personal and property crime, and within each offence category, it seems likely that different sub-groups of the offence are affected differently. The likelihood that a given offence will lead to the offender

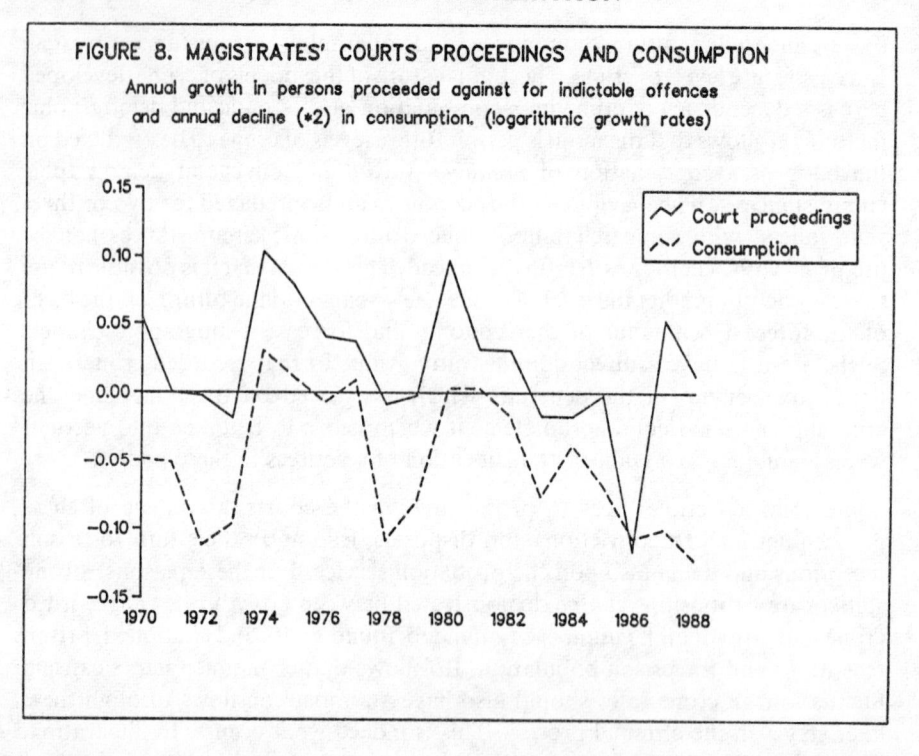

FIGURE 8. MAGISTRATES' COURTS PROCEEDINGS AND CONSUMPTION
Annual growth in persons proceeded against for indictable offences and annual decline (*2) in consumption. (logarithmic growth rates)

being brought to trial and convicted, and that the conviction will lead to custodial treatment or involvement in the probation system will depend on the nature of that offence. Moreover different offender groups are likely to respond in diverse ways to economic fluctuations. Second, economic factors may have a direct influence on flows through the criminal process. A number of research studies, including two conducted in this country, have suggested that the level of unemployment increases the proportion of persons who, on conviction, are sentenced to custody (Hale, 1989, Sabol 1989). If this is so, it suggests a separate source of economic influence on prison receptions.

Analysis of this type could also be conducted on local patterns of crime, for example, in one police force area. Economic data is not readily available for police force areas, but it is available for regions, providing some measure of the economic influences operating in that part of the country. Demographic information can also be related to police force areas. This would allow a broadly similar approach to the interpretation of trends in crime in individual police force areas as has been followed here on England and Wales. Within such a framework, individual police forces could interpret and perhaps forecast trends in local patterns in crime. Moreover the patterns in different force areas would

CONCLUSION: IMPLICATIONS OF THE FINDINGS

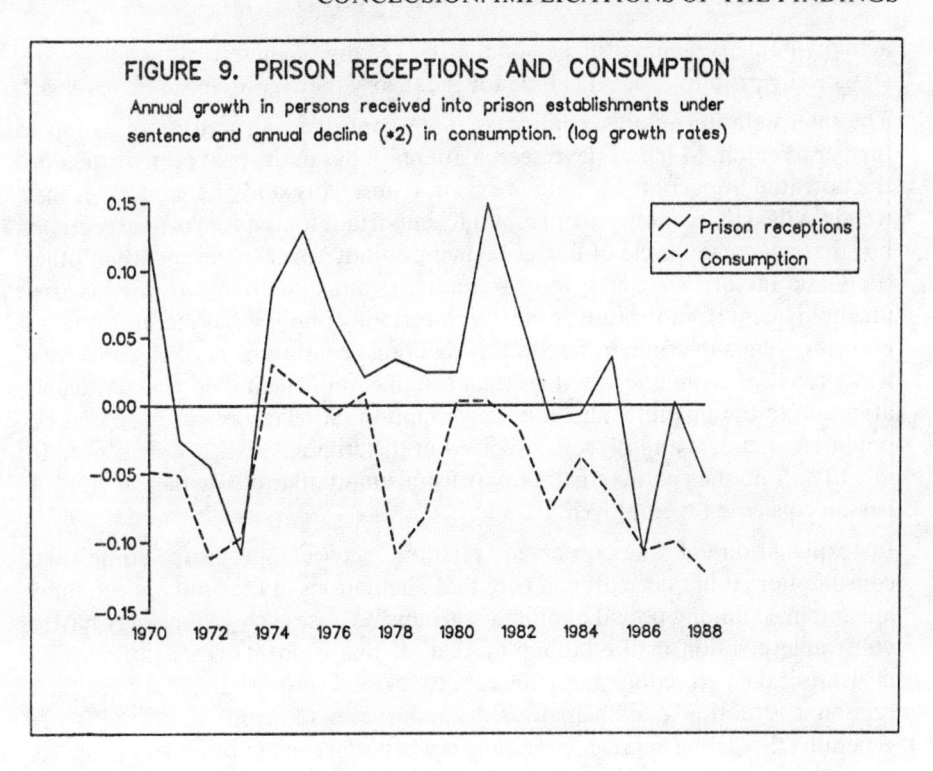

FIGURE 9. PRISON RECEPTIONS AND CONSUMPTION
Annual growth in persons received into prison establishments under sentence and annual decline (*2) in consumption. (log growth rates)

be subject to systematic comparisons, and this would provide a framework within which the impact of different policing strategies and different patterns of resource allocation might be assessed in terms of their impact on crime.

In addition to their immediate practical applications, these results have significant implications for an understanding of the social origins of crime and for criminological research on that topic. Orsagh and Witte (1981) summed up the recent research literature on the relation between economic status and crime, with a verdict of 'not proven'. The strength and generality of the relation between consumption growth and property crime revealed by this study requires a revision of this view. The behaviour of the economy clearly *does* affect the level of crime.

Curiously enough, the more recent agnosticism on crime and the economy, which has rested heavily on the failure to produce clear and consistent evidence of a relation between unemployment and crime, has eclipsed an older view, described in the previous chapter, stretching into the 19th century which asserted that economic downturns detrimentally affect rates of property crime but may actually improve figures for personal crime. Many of these early studies were statistically primitive, but it is time for the theory they represent to be revived.

The interpretation of this relation is more controversial, and requires much further research. Much of the research attention has in the past been devoted to the potential impact of unemployment on crime. This study demonstrates that trends in the UK economy are profoundly important to trends in property crime, but that aggregate levels of unemployment do not appear relevant when other economic factors are taken into account. It does not follow from this that unemployment cannot cause crime, but it certainly implies that research studies covering trends in crime in relation to economic conditions need to consider a wider range of economic variables than just unemployment, and give particular attention to the possible impact of consumption. Similarly research studies on potential offenders and persons involved in the criminal justice system need to identify economic characteristics apart from simply that of whether or not the person concerned is employed.

In explanation of the observed relation between property crime and consumption, it has been argued here that fluctuations in the national economy are amplified among potential offender groups because such groups may have a vulnerable position in the labour market. If this is so, it would follow that measures taken to reduce the vulnerability of such groups and improve their economic situation may help to reduce the level of property crime. More generally, the strong aggregate relationship between consumption and property crime must, at bottom, be explicable in terms of a relationship between the economic status of individuals and their propensity to become involved in crime. It may be that persons who face sudden reverses in their economic circumstances are particularly likely to become involved in crime. This study has identified aggregate indicators of this effect, and it would be consistent with these findings to suppose that such individual reverses are a continuous factor behind the level of property crime, and not simply an explanation which only has relevance to the impact of national economic trends.

Findings at this level of generality are at some remove from specific policy prescriptions, but they support the proposition that measures to support the economic position of individuals, social groups or localities who are identified as 'at risk' could reduce the total amount of property crime. The particular emphasis suggested by these findings lies with the pattern over time of the economic circumstances leading to crime. The implication is that sudden reverses in circumstances, rather than simply poor economic circumstances, may lie behind the commission of crime. This implies that economic interventions which aim (perhaps among other objectives) to reduce the level of property crime, should seek to *secure* as well as improving the economic position of individuals at risk.

The identified relation between personal crime and consumption does not lend itself as readily to policy prescription. The underlying factor is almost certainly

CONCLUSION: IMPLICATIONS OF THE FINDINGS

for persons to spend increased income on leisure activities away from home where their risk of victimisation is higher. However the findings relating beer consumption to offences of violence against the person must give rise to concern. It does not appear that alcohol as such is related to the level of violent crime. A closer scrutiny is required of the mix of alcohol and social circumstances which are related to such crimes, and the other factors, including the price of alcoholic drinks, licensing hours, the terms and conditions of licences and the location of licensed premises which appear to be particularly relevant.

In conclusion, the findings of this research study have immediate practical and theoretical application. On the practical side, there has emerged a novel means of looking at crime statistics in relation to trends in the economy. This provides a means of understanding some of the major features of crime trends and anticipating their course a few years into the future. This has great practical value as a means of forecasting demands on the criminal justice system.

On the theoretical side, strong evidence has emerged of economic causes of crime. The precise nature of these causes deserves to be further unravelled, and further research in this field could yield evidence of the scope for initiatives and policies designed to mitigate the criminogenic impact of these economic causes.

Appendix A: the regression results

The tables that follow quote the first stage and final regression results for each of the twelve chosen categories of crime.

The results quoted in the main part of the tables include the *estimated coefficient* on the regressor, which is an indication of the estimated magnitude of the statistical relationship between the regressor and the dependent crime variable, the associated *standard error*, which is an indicator of the reliability of that estimate, and the *t-ratio*, which is a test of the hypothesis that there is no statistical relationship between the regressor and the dependent variable. Values of the t-ratio greater than about 1.8 (dependent on the number of variables and sample size) indicate that a significant relationship has been identified. The *R-squared* value, the *Standard Error of the Regression*, and the *Maximum of the Log-Likelihood* are all measures of the 'fit' of the regression. The *Durbin-Watson statistic* is a test of first order serial correlation, but in most cases it is of informal rather than formal significance, since it is not strictly applicable to regressions including a lagged dependent variable as one of the regressors.

Mis-specification tests

The mis-specification tests quoted for the final regressions are designed to test the validity of the assumptions underlying the statistical model which underpins inferences drawn from the regression results. These assumptions are spelt out in detail in Spanos (1986).

The test for *serial correlation* quoted is that described by Godfrey (1978) for serial correlation in the residuals, in its F-statistic version.

The test for *functional form* is Ramsey's RESET test (Ramsey, 1969). An auxiliary regression is carried out in which the square of fitted values of the dependent variable is included as an additional regressor. This implicitly tests the possibility that higher powers or cross-products of the original regressors are relevant.

The test for *normality* is that described by Jarque and Bera (1980). This tests whether the skewness and kurtosis of the distribution of the regression residuals are those expected under normality.

The test for *heteroscedasticity* derives from an auxiliary regression in which the dependent variable is the square of the residual, and the regressors include the square of the fitted value and a constant. A test is run on whether the estimated coefficient on the squared fitted value is non-zero. (See Koenker, 1981).

APPENDIX A: THE REGRESSION RESULTS

The *structural stability* tests are computed by splitting the data at 1969, and comparing regressions for the two sub-samples to determine whether the variance or the coefficients vary over the whole period. Initially a test was conducted for variance equality over the two sub-periods, as described by Spanos (1986), and all the regression models passed this test. The test results quoted depend on the assumption of variance equality over the two sub-periods. One function of the structural stability tests will be to identify any changes resulting from the altered data basis following the introduction of the Theft Act 1968.

The *predictive failure* test is the second test described by Chow (1960), which simultaneously tests for variance and coefficient equality over the two sub-periods.

The *coefficient stability* test is the first test described by Chow (1960), and tests the equality of regression coefficients over the two sub-periods conditional on the equality of error variances.

Table A.1
Residential burglary

Regressions using RESIDENTIAL BURGLARY as the dependent variable

Sample period	First stage regression 1952 to 1987			Final regression 1953 to 1987		
Regressor	coeff.	S. E.	T-ratio	coeff.	S. E.	T-ratio
INTERCEPT	·009	·027	·344	−·107	·070	−1·517
CONVICTED(−1)	·659	·176	3·745	·592	·138	4·278
CONSUMPTION	−·996	·604	−1·647	−1·369	·566	−2·418
CONSUMPTION(−2)	1·936	·654	2·956	1·344	·542	2·476
WEATHER	−·089	·039	−2·288	−·090	·030	−2·967
LIVE BIRTHS(−1)				·686	·251	2·728
R. BURGLARY (−4)	−·233	·123	−1·897	−·233	·094	−2·465
TREND				·045	·019	2·290
MALES 15-19	·946	·391	2·418	·672	·334	2·013
MALES 20-24	1·467	·506	2·894	·938	·472	1·987
Residuals:						
SHOP THEFT(−1)				·699	·246	2·835
CRIMINAL DAMAGE(−1)				−·414	·197	−2·101
THEFT FROM THE PERSON(−1)				−·214	·103	−2·082
R-Squared	·690			·876		
S.E. of regression	·056			·040		
Maximum of Log-likelihood	56·887			70·830		
DW-statistic	2·018			2·462		
Mis-specification tests						
serial correlation				1·49	(F,1,21)	
functional form				1·25	(F,1,21)	
normality				0·23	(chi-sq,2)	
heteroscedasticity				1·31	(F,1,33)	
structural stability tests splitting data at 1969:						
predictive failure				2·82	(F,18,4)	
coefficient stability				0·94	(F,13,9)	

All variables apart from intercept, trend and residuals are growth rates (first logarithmic differences).

All t-ratios for coefficients apart from the intercept in final regression are significant at the 5 per cent level. None of the mis-specification tests were significant at the 5 per cent level.

APPENDIX A: THE REGRESSION RESULTS

Table A.2

Non-residential burglary

Regressions using NON-RESIDENTIAL BURGLARY as the dependent variable

Sample period	First stage regression 1952 to 1987			Final regression 1953 to 1987		
Regressor	coeff.	S. E.	T-ratio	coeff.	S. E.	T-ratio
INTERCEPT	·013	·028	·467	−·195	·094	−2·083
CONSUMPTION	−1·878	·642	−2·921	−2·300	·656	−3·501
CONSUMPTION(−2)	2·808	·734	3·826	3·099	·626	4·948
N. R. BURGLARY(−4)	−·227	·111	−2·030	−·347	·097	−3·576
DUMMY(1980)	−·124	·070	−1·774	−·217	·061	−3·552
WEATHER	−·128	·042	−3·039	−·112	·036	−3·097
LIVE BIRTHS(−1)				·992	·351	2·821
TREND				·070	·026	2·651
MALES 15-19	1·292	·426	3·031	·980	·389	2·515
MALES 20-24	1·674	·555	3·015	1·069	·539	1·981
Residuals:						
RESIDENTIAL BURGLARY(−1)				−·883	·229	−3·845
OTHER THEFT(−1)				1·463	·418	3·497
THEFT FROM THE PERSON(−1)				−·238	·115	−2·060

R-Squared	·685	·853
S.E. of regression	·062	·048
Maximum of Log-likelihood	52·997	64·644
DW-statistic	1·927	2·235
Mis-specification tests		
serial correlation		0·57 (F,1,21)
functional form		0·94 (F,1,21)
normality		1·54 (chi-sq,2)
heteroscedasticity		0·01 (F,1,33)
structural stability tests splitting data at 1969:		
predictive failure		1·41 (F,18,5)
coefficient stability		1·89 (F,12,11)

All variables apart from intercept, trend and residuals are growth rates (first logarithmic differences).

All t-ratios for coefficients apart from the intercept in final regression are significant at the 5 per cent level. None of the mis-specification tests were significant at the 5 per cent level.

TRENDS IN CRIME AND THEIR INTERPRETATION

Table A.3

Theft from the person

Regressions using THEFT FROM THE PERSON as the dependent variable

Sample period	First stage regression 1952 to 1987			Final regression 1953 to 1987		
Regressor	coeff.	S. E.	T-ratio	coeff.	S. E.	T-ratio
INTERCEPT	·122	·035	3·466	·015	·019	·757
CONSUMPTION(−3)				1·953	·741	2·636
DUMMY (1969)	−·254	·091	−2·771			
CONSUMPTION	−2·847	·875	−3·251			
MALES 25-29	2·059	·751	2·740			
POLICE	−1·016	·992	−1·024			
THEFT/PERSON(−3)	·274	·151	1·812			
MALES 10-14	·816	·498	1·637			
MALES 15-19				·922	·514	1·790
Residuals:						
THEFT FROM VEHICLE(−1)				−·768	·305	−2·519
THEFT OF VEHICLE(−1)				−·996	·398	−2·497

R-Squared	·395	·435
S.E. of regression	·083	·078
Maximum of Log-likelihood	42·118	41·976
DW-statistic	1·979	1·351
Mis-specification tests		
serial correlation		3·66 (F,1,29)
functional form		(S)8·74 (F,1,29)
normality		2·53 (chi-sq,2)
heteroscedasticity		(S)6·48 (F,1,33)
structural stability tests		
splitting data at 1969:		
predictive failure		0·87 (F,18,12)
coefficient stability		1·58 (F,5,25)

All variables apart from intercept, trend and residuals are growth rates (first logarithmic differences).

All t-ratios for coefficients apart from the intercept in final regression are significant at 5 per cent level. None of the mis-specification tests were significant at the 5 per cent level except those indicated by (S).

APPENDIX A: THE REGRESSION RESULTS

Table A.4

Shop theft

Regressions using SHOP THEFT as the dependent variable

Sample period	First stage regression 1952 to 1986			Final regression 1953 to 1987		
Regressor	coeff.	S. E.	T-ratio	coeff.	S. E.	T-ratio
INTERCEPT	·135	·023	5·805	·153	·022	6·760
CONSUMPTION	−3·090	·478	−6·466	−3·146	·513	−6·128
CONSUMPTION (−3)	−1·531	·545	−2·808	−1·791	·437	−4·099
DUMMY (1980)	−·076	·052	−1·458	−·169	·043	−3·854
MALES 10-14	1·723	·338	5·085	·954	·285	3·348
MALES 15-19	1·446	·311	4·644	·729	·302	2·410
MALES 20-24	1·371	·424	3·228	·353	·447	·790
MALES 25-29	2·325	·381	6·103	1·528	·387	3·941
WEATHER	−·072	·027	−2·616	−·061	·025	−2·370
LIVE BIRTHS (−2)				·523	·232	2·253
POLICE	−1·333	·595	−2·240			
POLICE (−1)	−·612	·521	−1·175			
SHOP THEFT (−4)	·122	·107	1·139			
PRISONERS	·274	·179	1·531			
Residuals:						
NON-RESIDENTIAL BURGLARY (−1)				·497	·153	3·234
R. BURGLARY (−1)				−·377	·177	−2·129
CRIMINAL DAMAGE (−1)				−·319	·167	−1·904

R-Squared	·822	·862
S.E. of regression	·040	·0354
Maximum of Log-likelihood	70·774	75·0418
DW-statistic	2·346	2·2642
Mis-specification tests		
serial correlation		2·51 (F,1,21)
functional form		0·86 (F,1,21)
normality		1·44 (chi-sq,2)
heteroscedasticity		0·00 (F,1,33)
structural stability tests splitting data at 1969:		
predictive failure		2·02 (F,18,5)
coefficient stability		1·09 (F,12,11)

All variables apart from intercept, trend and residuals are growth rates (first logarithmic differences).

All t-ratios for coefficients apart from the intercept and that for males aged 20-24 in the final regression are significant at the 5 per cent level. None of the mis-specification tests were significant at the 5 per cent level.

TRENDS IN CRIME AND THEIR INTERPRETATION

Table A.5

Theft of vehicle

Regressions using THEFT OF VEHICLE as the dependent variable

Sample period	First stage regression estimated as an AR1 process 1952 to 1986			Final regression 1952 to 1987		
Regressor	coeff.	S. E.	T-ratio	coeff.	S. E.	T-ratio
INTERCEPT	−·310	·208	−1·486	·019	·029	·665
TREND	·090	·058	1·544			
UNEMPLOYMENT	−·121	·060	−2·016			
NEW CARS	−·099	·096	−1·028			
PRISONERS(−1)	·919	·258	3·557			
CONSUMPTION	−3·234	·760	−4·252	−3·033	·643	−4·715
CONVICTED(T)(−1)	1·673	·231	7·232	1·929	·272	7·071
MALES (10−14)	1·887	·310	6·081	1·266	·379	3·337
CARS	1·815	·566	3·204	·929	·338	2·743
POLICE	−2·411	·611	−3·942	−2·929	·793	−3·693
CLEAR-UP(T)(−1)	−2·014	·320	−6·280	−1·566	·345	−4·529
CONSUMPTION(−1)	4·241	·880	4·818	5·217	·780	6·687
VEHICLE THEFT(−4)	−·216	·050	−4·278	−·137	·061	−2·251
VEHICLE THEFT(−2)	−·270	·091	−2·968	−·269	·082	−3·255
DUMMY (1969)				−·095	·068	−1·404

R-Squared	·891	·788
S.E. of Regression	·048	·061
Maximum of Log-likelihood	66·141	55·80
DW-statistic	2·291	2·523
Mis-specification tests		
serial correlation		2·96 (F,1,24)
functional form		0·34 (F,1,24)
normality		1·26 (chi-sq,2)
heteroscedasticity		0·03 (F,1,34)
structural stability tests splitting data at 1969:		
predictive failure		4·71 (F,19,7)(s)
coefficient stability		1·52 (F,10,16)

All variables apart from intercept, trend and residuals are growth rates (first logarithmic differences).

All t-ratios for coefficients apart from the intercept and that for the 1969 dummy were significant at the 5 per cent level. None of the mis-specification tests were significant at the 5 per cent level except for that for predictive failure indicated by (S).

APPENDIX A: THE REGRESSION RESULTS

Table A.6

Theft from vehicle

Regressions using **THEFT FROM VEHICLE** as the dependent variable

Sample period	First stage regression 1952 to 1986			Final regression 1953 to 1987		
Regressor	coeff.	S. E.	T-ratio	coeff.	S. E.	T-ratio
INTERCEPT	−·314	·196	−1·599	·118	·024	4·824
LIVE BIRTHS(−2)				1·369	·241	5·676
CONSUMPTION	−2·717	·841	−3·230	−1·091	·529	−2·060
CONSUMPTION(−3)	1·820	·656	2·772	1·689	·479	3·526
CONSUMPTION(−4)				·916	·459	1·995
POLICE	−2·515	·733	−3·430	−1·268	·579	−2·190
POLICE(−1)	−1·768	·775	−2·280	−2·201	·573	−3·836
MALES 15−19	1·155	·403	2·865	·707	·299	2·361
DUMMY (1969)				−·159	·049	−3·229
TREND	·114	·053	2·150			
CARS	1·700	·563	3·018			
PRISONERS(−1)	·597	·262	2·276			
U. BENEFIT	·323	·219	1·474			
NEW CARS	−·145	·115	−1·262			
Residuals:						
NON-RESIDENTIAL BURGLARY(−1)				·766	·189	4·039
R. BURGLARY(−1)				−·813	·208	−3·897
THEFT OF VEHICLE(−1)				−·580	·241	−2·397
CRIMINAL DAMAGE(−1)				−·387	·210	−1·840

R-Squared	·689	·840
S.E. of regression	·058	·042
Maximum of Log-likelihood	56·383	68·933
DW-statistic	1·870	2·221
Mis-specification tests		
serial correlation		0·87 (F,1,21)
functional form		0.37 (F,1,21)
normality		1·36 (chi-sq,2)
heteroscedasticity		0·29 (F,1,33)
structural stability tests		
splitting data at 1969:		
predictive failure		1·27 (F,18,4)
coefficient stability		not applicable

All variables apart from intercept, trend and residuals are growth rates (first logarithmic differences).

All t-ratios for coefficients apart from the intercept in final regression were significant at the five per cent level. None of the mis-specification tests were significant at the five per cent level.

TRENDS IN CRIME AND THEIR INTERPRETATION

Table A.7

Other theft

Regressions using OTHER THEFT as the dependent variable

Sample period	First stage regression 1952 to 1987			Final regression 1953 to 1987		
Regressor	coeff.	S. E.	T-ratio	coeff.	S. E.	T-ratio
INTERCEPT	·016	·015	1·057	·011	·014	·830
CONSUMPTION	−1·678	·322	−5·213	−1·819	·265	−6·855
CONSUMPTION(−1)	1·544	·398	3·877	1·939	·334	5·799
CONSUMPTION(−4)				·776	·262	2·956
CONVICTED(TH)(−1)	·426	·122	3·478	·631	·099	6.366
CLEAR-UP(TH)(−1)	−·533	·164	−3·238	−·524	·148	−3·522
POLICE	−1·231	·392	−3·137	−·834	·346	−2·405
MALES 20-24	1·399	·301	4·644	·432	·224	1·928
OTHER THEFT(−3)	−·142	·094	−1·507	−·156	·083	−1·870
MALES 10-14	·583	·208	2·795			
MALES 15-19	·808	·231	3·488			
MALES 25-29	·576	·276	2·083			
Residuals:						
THEFT FROM THE PERSON(−1)				−·151	·069	−2·176

R-Squared	·788	·838
S.E. of regression	·030	·026
Maximum of Log-likelihood	81·164	83·922
DW-statistic	2·430	2·427
Mis-specification tests		
serial correlation		1·62 (F,1,24)
functional form		0.01 (F,1,24)
normality		0·06 (chi-sq,2)
heteroscedasticity		0·73 (F,1,33)
structural stability tests splitting data at 1969:		
predictive failure		3·60 (F,18,7)
coefficient stability		1·47 (F,12,11)

All variables apart from intercept, trend and residuals are growth rates (first logarithmic differences).

All the t-ratios for coefficients apart from the intercept in the final regression were significant at the 5 per cent level. None of the mis-specification tests were significant at the 5 per cent level.

APPENDIX A: THE REGRESSION RESULTS

Table A.8

Robbery

Regressions using ROBBERY as the dependent variable

Sample period	First stage regression 1952 to 1987			Final regression 1953 to 1987		
Regressor	coeff.	S. E.	T-ratio	coeff.	S. E.	T-ratio
INTERCEPT	·135	·035	3·773	·140	·024	5·699
CONSUMPTION	−3·196	·888	−3·595	−2·955	·621	−4·757
CONSUMPTION (−3)				2·346	·621	3·777
LIVE BIRTHS (−1)				1·084	·306	3·535
ROBBERY (−4)	−·327	·113	−2·889	−·201	·078	−2·573
CONVICTED (−1)	·753	·236	3·180			
MALES 25-29	1·204	·755	1·594			
CONSUMPTION (−2)	1·813	·851	2·129			
Residuals:						
NON-RESIDENTIAL BURGLARY (−1)				·918	·191	4·805
THEFT OF VEHICLE (−1)				−1·324	·311	−4·247

R-Squared	·618	·795
S.E. of regression	·081	·060
Maximum of Log-likelihood	42·470	52·252
DW-statistic	1·707	2·476
Mis-specification tests		
serial correlation		3·29 (F,1,27)
functional form		0·23 (F,1,27)
normality		0·17 (chi-sq,2)
heteroscedasticity		2·64 (F,1,33)
structural stability tests		
splitting data at 1969:		
predictive failure		0·74 (F,18,10)
coefficient stability		1·44 (F,7,21)

All variables apart from intercept, trend and residuals are growth rates (first logarithmic differences).

All the t-ratios for coefficients apart from the intercept in the final regression were significant at the 5 per cent level. None of the mis-specification tests were significant at the 5 per cent level.

Table A.9

Violence against the person

Regressions using VIOLENCE AGAINST THE PERSON as the dependent variable

Sample period	First stage regression 1952 to 1987			Final regression 1953 to 1987		
Regressor	coeff.	S. E.	T-ratio	coeff.	S. E.	T-ratio
INTERCEPT	·120	·039	3·065	·195	·044	4·351
BEER CONSUMPTION	1·215	·174	6·980	1·132	·132	8·531
CONSUMPTION(−1)	1·021	·235	4·330	1·211	·200	6·037
CONSUMPTION(−3)	·620	·242	2·557	·896	·177	5·048
UNEMPLOYMENT(−1)	·106	·022	4·802	·108	·017	6.227
U BENEFIT				−·188	·073	−2·580
U BENEFIT(−1)				−·213	·082	−2·583
VIOLENCE/PERSON(-3)	−·336	·097	−3·466	−·311	·074	−4·199
TREND	−·024	·011	−2·121	−·044	·012	−3·658
MALES 10-14	·480	·162	2·961	·348	·136	2·554
CLEAR UP(−1)	−·388	·131	−2·964	−·230	·108	−2·129
POLICE	·962	·323	2·977	·458	·253	1·806
Residuals:						
NON-RESIDENTIAL BURGLARY(−1)				·299	·060	4·995
SEXUAL OFFENCES(−1)				·265	·111	−2·370
SHOP THEFT(−1)				−·183	·094	−1·936

R-Squared	·824	·939
S.E. of regression	·022	·015
Maximum of Log-likelihood	91·336	107·043
DW-statistic	2·486	2·237
Mis-specification tests		
serial correlation		0·53 (F,1,19)
functional form		0·70 (F,1,19)
normality		0·88 (chi-sq,2)
heteroscedasticity		1·11 (F,1,33)
structural stability tests splitting data at 1969:		
predictive failure		7·66 (F,18,2)
coefficient stability		(S)7·10 (F,15,5)

All variables apart from intercept, trend and residuals are growth rates (first logarithmic differences).

All the t-ratios for coefficients apart from the intercept in the final regression are significant at the 5 per cent level. None of the mis-specification tests were significant at the 5 per cent level except that indicated by (S).

APPENDIX A: THE REGRESSION RESULTS

Table A.10

Sexual offences

Regressions using SEXUAL OFFENCES as the dependent variable

Sample period	First stage regression 1952 to 1987			Final regression 1953 to 1987		
Regressor	coeff.	S. E.	T-ratio	coeff.	S. E.	T-ratio
INTERCEPT	·039	·060	·650	−·031	·016	−1·930
CONSUMPTION	1·629	·377	4·321	1·255	·346	3·620
CONSUMPTION (−2)	·845	·360	2·344	·936	·299	3·123
SEXUAL OFFENCES (−4)	·190	·139	1·361	·327	·098	3·310
WEATHER	·053	·022	2·356	·059	·020	2.956
MALES 20-24	·736	·275	2·677	·754	·258	2·923
POLICE				−·843	·365	−2·305
TREND	−·022	·017	−1·307			
UNEMPLOYMENT	−·048	·033	−1·455			
CONSUMPTION (−1)	−·712	·406	−1·753			
Residuals:						
CRIMINAL DAMAGE (−1)				·266	·135	1·963
ROBBERY (−1)				·148	·079	1·871

R-Squared	·661	·765
S.E. of regression	·032	·028
Maximum of Log-likelihood	75·722	80·519
DW-statistic	1·736	1·664
Mis-specification tests		
serial correlation		0·25 (F,1,25)
functional form		0·80 (F,1,25)
normality		0·67 (chi-sq,2)
heteroscedasticity		0·89 (F,1,33)
structural stability tests splitting data at 1969:		
predictive failure		0·48 (F,18,8)
coefficient stability		0·70 (F,9,17)

All variables apart from intercept, trend and residuals are growth rates (first logarithmic differences).

All t-ratios for coefficients apart from the intercept in the final regression were significant at the 5 per cent level. None of the mis-specification tests were significant at the 5 per cent level.

TRENDS IN CRIME AND THEIR INTERPRETATION

Table A.11

Criminal damage

Regressions using CRIMINAL DAMAGE as dependent variable

Sample period	First stage regression 1952 to 1987			Final regression 1953 to 1987		
Regressor	coeff.	S. E.	T-ratio	coeff.	S. E.	T-ratio
INTERCEPT	−·339	·127	−2·662	−·086	·118	−·724
CONSUMPTION	−2·638	·821	−3·212	−3·057	·794	−3·847
CONSUMPTION (−3)	−1·804	·587	−3·071	−1·811	·554	−3·270
MALES 10-14	2·249	·398	5·645	1·550	·428	3·617
MALES 15-19	1·294	·393	3·291	·958	·420	2·279
MALES 20-24	−1·381	·634	−2·178	−2·138	·632	−3·382
MALES 25-29	1·909	·578	3·302	1·603	·464	3·454
TREND	·177	·046	3·813	·105	·033	3·207
CLEAR UP (CD)(−2)	−·381	·158	−2·406	−·618	·150	−4·111
PRISONERS (−1)	·498	·199	2·498	·568	·188	3·021
CRIMINAL DAMAGE (−3)				−·214	·116	−1·842
INFLATION	−·543	·382	−1·419			
Residuals:						
NON-RESIDENTIAL BURGLARY (−1)				·475	·172	2·751
THEFT FROM VEHICLE (−1)				−·562	·216	−2·602
SHOP THEFT (−1)				·614	·279	2·195

R-Squared	·764	·856
S.E. of regression	·052	·043
Maximum of Log-likelihood	61·561	69·393
DW-statistic	2·420	2·617
Mis-specification tests		
serial correlation		3·77 (F,1,20)
functional form		2·81 (F,1,20)
normality		1·18 (chi-sq,2)
heteroscedasticity		(S)4·38 (F,1,33)
structural stability tests splitting data at 1969:		
predictive failure		0·70 (F,18,3)
coefficient stability		0·77 (F,14,7)

All variables apart from intercept, trend and residuals are growth rates (first logarithmic differences).

All t-ratios for coefficients apart from the intercept in the final regression were significant at the 5 per cent level. None of the mis-specification tests were significant at the 5 per cent level except that indicated by (S).

APPENDIX A: THE REGRESSION RESULTS

Table A.12
Fraud
Regressions using FRAUD as the dependent variable

Sample period	First stage regression 1952 to 1987			Final regression 1952 to 1987		
Regressor	coeff.	S. E.	T-ratio	coeff.	S. E.	T-ratio
INTERCEPT	·034	·020	1·683	·030	·016	1·904
MALES 10-14	·944	·349	2·702	1·073	·336	3·190
MALES 15-19	·599	·385	1·556	·745	·362	2·059
MALES 20-24	1·267	·475	2·664	1·335	·467	2·855
MALES 25-29	1·691	·479	3·524	1·846	·444	4.155
CONSUMPTION(−1)				−1·174	·488	−2·403
DUMMY (1969)	−·154	·074	−2·061			
DUMMY (1980)	−·079	·057	−1·395			
CONSUMPTION	−·860	·532	−1·616			
CONVICTED(FR)(−1)	·432	·179	2·412			
FRAUD(−1)	·244	·156	1·431			
POLICE(−1)	−1·057	·752	−1·405			
FRAUD(−2)	−·209	·154	−1·356			
R-Squared		·613			·470	
S.E. of regression		·050			·053	
Maximum of Log-likelihood		63·508			57·803	
DW-statistic		2·144			1·869	
Mis-specification tests						
serial correlation				0·07	(F,1,29)	
functional form				1·26	(F,1,29)	
normality				4·85	(chi-sq,2)	
heteroscedasticity				0·16	(F,1,34)	
structural stability tests splitting data at 1969:						
predictive failure				0·46	(F,18,12)	
coefficient stability				0·94	(F,6,24)	

All variables apart from intercept, trend and residuals are growth rates (first logarithmic differences).

All t-ratios for coefficients apart from the intercept in the final regression are significant at the 5 per cent level. None of the mis-specification tests were significant at the 5 per cent level.

Appendix B: the data

RECORDED CRIME CATEGORIES.

Figures in brackets indicate crime categories.

RESIDENTIAL BURGLARY

(1) Prior to 1969, housebreaking. (2) Since 1969 burglary in a dwelling (categories 28 and 29).

Note: the growth variable for 1969 was spliced.

Source: Criminal Statistics.

NON-RESIDENTIAL BURGLARY

(1) Prior to 1969, shop-breaking. (2) Since 1969 burglary not in a dwelling (categories 28 and 29).

Note: the growth variable for 1969 was spliced.

Source: Criminal Statistics.

THEFT/LARCENY FROM THE PERSON (39)

Source: Criminal Statistics.

THEFT/LARCENY FROM SHOPS (46)

Source: Criminal Statistics.

THEFT OF VEHICLE (48)

Source: Criminal Statistics.

Note: up to 1969 many offences in this category were not indictable, the growth variable for 1969 was spliced.

THEFT FROM A VEHICLE (45)

Source: Criminal Statistics.

Note: the growth variable for 1969 was spliced.

OTHER THEFT (40-44, 47, 49, 54)

This variable is defined as all theft and handling/larceny minus shop theft and theft from a person and theft of and from a vehicle.

Note: the growth variable for 1969 was spliced.

ROBBERY (34)

Source: Criminal Statistics.

APPENDIX B: THE DATA

VIOLENCE AGAINST THE PERSON, including wounding, assault and homicide (1-15).
Source: Criminal Statistics.

SEXUAL OFFENCES (16-26, 74)
Source: Criminal Statistics.

CRIMINAL DAMAGE (56-59 in latest series)
Criminal damage and arson excluding offences of criminal damage of value under £20.
Source: Criminal Statistics.

FRAUD (51-53 & 50 prior to 1969)
Fraud by company director etc., false accounting and other fraud.
Source: Criminal Statistics.

INDEPENDENT VARIABLES

ALCOHOL CONSUMPTION
Pints per head by type of alcohol: beer and other.
Source: The Brewer's Society Statistics Handbook.

BEER CONSUMPTION
Beer production released for home consumption by volume.
Source: Annual Abstract of Statistics.

CARS
Private vehicles with current licenses in Great Britain.
Note: there is no data for 1977 due to a change in the recording procedure. The growth variables for 1977 and 1978 were spliced.
Source: Annual Abstract of Statistics.

CLEAR UP

CLEAR UP (CRIMINAL DAMAGE)
CLEAR UP (THEFT AND LARCENY)
The ratio of notifiable crimes cleared to all notifiable crime in the category.
Source: Criminal Statistics.

CONSUMERS EXPENDITURE ON DURABLES.
UK Consumer expenditure on durable goods at 1980 prices.
Source: Economic Trends Annual Supplement.

TRENDS IN CRIME AND THEIR INTERPRETATION

CONSUMPTION: PERSONAL CONSUMPTION PER CAPITA
UK Personal expenditure per capita at 1980 prices.
Source: Economic Trends Annual Supplement.

CONTENTS INSURANCE
Percentage of households recording expenditure on contents insurance.
Source: Family Expenditure Survey.

CONTENTS INSURANCE EXPENDITURE
Average weekly household expenditure for insurance of contents of dwelling (divided by **RPI** to yield real expenditure).
Source: Family Expenditure Survey.

CONVICTED

CONVICTED (CRIMINAL DAMAGE)

CONVICTED (FRAUD)

CONVICTED (SEXUAL OFFENCES)

CONVICTED (THEFT AND LARCENY)

CONVICTED (VIOLENCE AGAINST THE PERSON)
Offenders found guilty or cautioned for indictable offences in the relevant category.
Note: the growth rate variables were spliced in 1969 and 1977-78 to take account of definitional changes.
Source: Criminal Statistics.

CONVICTED (FRAUD)
Offenders found guilty or cautioned for offences of fraud and forgery.
Note: the growth rate variable was spliced in 1969 and 1977-78 to take account of definitional changes.
Source: Criminal Statistics.

CONVICTED (CRIMINAL DAMAGE)
Offenders found guilty or cautioned for offences of criminal damage.
Note: the growth rate variable was spliced in 1969 and 1977-78 to take account of definitional changes.
Source: Criminal Statistics.

APPENDIX B: THE DATA

CONVICTED (THEFT AND LARCENY)

Offenders found guilty or cautioned for offences of theft and handling (larceny prior to 1969).

Note: the growth rate variable was spliced in 1969 and 1977-78 to take account of definitional changes. Offences of abstracting electricity were only included in the category from 1978 onwards.

Source: Criminal Statistics.

GROSS DOMESTIC PRODUCT

Gross Domestic Product per capita at factor cost at 1980 prices.

Source: Economic Trends Annual Supplement.

LICENCES

Number of full on-licences and off-licences in England and Wales.

Source: Brewer's Society Statistical Handbook.

LIVE BIRTHS

Number of live births in England and Wales.

Source: Annual Abstract of Statistics.

MALES 10-14

MALES 15-19

MALES 25-29

MALES 20-24

Age distribution of the home (resident) population of England and Wales at mid-year.

Source: Annual Abstract of Statistics.

NEW CARS

New private vehicle registrations in Great Britain.

Note: the growth variable was spliced for 1979 as a change in the counting procedure was introduced in that year.

Source: Annual Abstract of Statistics.

PERSONAL DISPOSAL INCOME PER CAPITA

Personal disposable income per capita at 1980 prices.

Source: Economic Trends Annual Supplement.

TRENDS IN CRIME AND THEIR INTERPRETATION

POLICE

Police strength (officers in post) in England and Wales.

Source: Annual Abstract of Statistics.

PRISON POPULATION

Persons in custody (sentenced and unsentenced).

Source: Annual Abstract of Statistics.

PRISON RECEPTIONS

Receptions of persons into custody under sentence, including receptions into youth custody, detention centres and borstal, and including fine defaulters.

Note: the figures from 1983 onwards reflect the effect of the Criminal Justice Act 1982.

Source: Annual Abstract of Statistics.

PROCEEDINGS IN MAGISTRATES' COURTS

Defendants proceeded against in magistrates' courts for indictable offences.

Note: a double counting problem was resolved from 1977 onwards. The data series prior to 1977 was adjusted to reflect the estimated effect of this change.

Source: Criminal Statistics.

SUPPLEMENTARY BENEFIT

(1) Prior to 1973 weekly scale rate of requirement other than for rent. (2) Since 1973 ordinary rate for married couples. Real supplementary benefit is defined as supplementary benefit divided by the RPI for that year.

Note: the growth variable for 1973 was spliced.

Source: Annual Abstract of Statistics.

TELEPHONES

Number of UK telephone stations at 31 March.

Source: Annual Abstract of Statistics.

TENURE

Estimated percentage of dwellings owner occupied at end-year: Great Britain.

Source: Annual Abstract of Statistics.

TREND

Defined as the logarithm to base e of t, where t is 1 for the first year in the sample, 2 for the second year in the sample etc.

APPENDIX B: THE DATA

UNEMPLOYMENT BENEFIT

Average UK weekly rate of unemployment benefit over year (divided by RPI to yield real unemployment benefit).

Source: Annual Abstract of Statistics.

UNEMPLOYMENT

Total UK employed including school leavers at mid-year.

Note: The earlier parts of the data series have been adjusted to take into account the estimated effects of (i) the 1983 change in the rules whereby some men over 60 were excluded from the figures, and (ii) the 1971 reorganisation of the data-collection around claimants at Unemployment Benefit offices.

Source: Annual Supplement of Economic Trends.

WEATHER

The ratio of mean daily sunshine to the annual total rainfall in millimetres in England and Wales.

Source: Annual Abstract of Statistics.

INTERNATIONAL DATA SOURCES

International consumption data

Real personal consumption figures are estimated as the ratio of nominal personal consumption to RPI.

Source: *International Financial Statistics: Supplement on Output Statistics,* IMF, Washington DC, 1984, and more recent editions of *International Financial Statistics*.

Long run data

This data is derived from Mitchell, B. R. (Ed.) *British Historical Statistics* Cambridge: Cambridge University Press.

Consumption expenditure is for the U.K. at constant prices. Unemployment data is for the U.K. In both cases the data is spliced at 1920 to reflect the exclusion of the South of Ireland from that date.

Property crime data is for indictable offences of property crime without violence known to the police. England and Wales.

International crime data

West Germany: the adjusted time series for serious crime quoted in *Economic Crisis and Crime,* Council of Europe, Strasbourg 1985, supplemented by *Polizeiliche Kriminalstatistik, 1985* Wiesbaden, 1986.

France: the time series for serious crime quoted in *Economic Crisis and Crime.*

TRENDS IN CRIME AND THEIR INTERPRETATION

The United States: Crime data property crime known to the police derived from *Sourcebook of Criminal Justice Statistics* (1988 and earlier editions), US Government Printing Office, Washington DC.

Sweden: Data for recorded theft. There were changes in statistical practices and a new penal code affecting data from 1965 onwards, changes in statistical practices affecting data from 1968 onwards, and from 1975 onwards.

Source: *Nordic Criminal Statistics 1950-80, 2nd revised edition* Stockholm, Statistics Sweden, 1983.

Japan: Data for the number of reported penal code offences other than traffic professional negligence.

Source: *Summary of The White Paper on Crime 1986* Tokyo: Ministry of Justice.

References

Ando, A. and Modigliani, F. (1963). 'The 'Life Cycle' hypothesis of saving: aggregate implications and tests' *American Economic Review* vol 53, pp. 55–84.

Becker, G. (1974). 'Crime and punishment: an economic approach' in *Essays in the Economics of Crime and Punishment* New York: National Bureau of Economic Research.

Bonger, W. (1916). *Criminality and Economic Conditions*. Chicago: Little and Brown.

Box, S. (1987). *Recession, Crime and Punishment* London: Macmillan.

Braithwaite, J. D. (1978). 'Unemployment and adult crime: an interpretation of the international evidence'. *Proceedings of the Institute of Criminology* pp. 54–68. University of Sydney, Australia.

Brenner, M. H. (1976). 'Effects of the economy on criminal behaviour and the administration of criminal justice in the United States, Canada, England and Wales and Scotland'. In *Economic Crisis and Crime*. Rome: UNSDRI.

Cantor, D. and Land, K. C. (1985). 'Unemployment and crime rates in the post-World War II United States: a theoretical and empirical analysis' *American Sociological Review* vol 50, pp. 317–332.

Carr-Hill, R. A. and Stern, N. H. (1979). *Crime, the Police and Criminal statistics*. London: Academic Press.

Chow, G. C. (1960). 'Tests of equality between sets of coefficients in two linear regressions'. *Econometrica,* vol 28, pp. 591–605.

Cohen, L. E., and Felson, M. (1979). 'Social change and crime rate trends: a routine activity approach' *American Sociological Review,* vol 44, pp. 588–608.

Davidoff, L. and Dowds, L. (1989). 'Recent trends in crimes of violence against the person in England and Wales' *Home Office Research Bulletin* 27, pp. 11–17.

Davies, J. C. (1969). 'The J-curve of rising and declining satisfactions as a cause of some great revolutions and a contained rebellion' in *Violence in America: Historical and Comparative Perspectives* edited by Graham, H. D. and Gurr, T. R., Washington: US Government Printing Office.

Doeringer, P. B. and Piore, M. J. (1985). *Internal Labour Markets and Manpower Analysis* London: M. E. Sharpe.

Easterlin, R. A. (1968). *Population, Labor Force and Long Swings in Economic Growth: The American Experience New York:* National Bureau of Economic Research.

Ehrlich, I. (1974). 'Participation in illegitimate activities: an economic analysis' in *Essays in the Economics of Crime and Punishment.* New York: National Bureau of Economic Research.

Farrington, D. P., Gallagher, B., Morley, L., St Ledger, R. J., and West, D. J. (1986). 'Unemployment, School Leaving, and Crime' *British Journal of Criminology* vol 26, 4, pp. 335–356.

Ferri, E. (1900). *Criminal Sociology* New York: Appleton, quoted in Vold, G. B., op cit.

Friedman, M. (1957). *A Theory of the Consumption Function.* Princeton: Princeton University Press.

Godfrey, L. G. (1978). 'Testing for higher order serial correlation in regression equations when the regressors include lagged dependent variables' *Econometrica* vol 46, pp. 1303–1310.

Hale, C. (1989). 'Unemployment, imprisonment, and the stability of punishment hypothesis: some results using cointegration and error correction models' *Journal of Quantitative Criminology* vol 5, no. 2. pp. 169–187.

Heineke, J. (1978). 'Economic models of criminal behaviour: an overview' in *Economic Models of Criminal Behavior* Oxford: North Holland.

Home Office. (1910). *Judicial Statistics, England and Wales, 1908* Part I—Criminal Statistics. London: HMSO.

Hough, M. and Mayhew, P. (1983). *The British Crime Survey.* Home Office Research Study No. 76. London: HMSO.

Jarque, C. M. and Bera, A. K. (1980). 'Efficient tests for normality, homoscedasticity and serial independence of regression residuals' *Economic Letters* 6, pp. 225–259.

Koenker, R. (1981). 'A note on studentizing a test for heteroscedasticity' *Econometrica*, vol 17, pp. 107–112.

Land, K. C. and Felson, M. (1986). 'A general framework for building dynamic macro social indicator models: including an analysis of changes in crime rates and police expenditures' *American Journal of Sociology*, vol 82, 3, pp. 565–604.

Lenke, L. (1982). 'Alcohol and crimes of violence: a causal analysis' *Contemporary Drug Problems*, Fall, 1982, pp. 355–367.

Lindbeck, A. and Snower, D. (1986). 'Wage setting, unemployment and insider-outsider relations' *American Economic Review, Papers and Proceedings*, vol 76, pp. 235–239.

REFERENCES

Long, S. K. and Witte, A. D. (1981). 'Current economic trends: implications for crime and criminal justice', in Wright, K. N. (Ed.) *Crime and Criminal Justice in a Declining Economy*. Cambridge, Mass: Oelgeschlager, Gunn and Hain.

Mannheim, H. (1965). *Comparative Criminology*. vol 2. London: Routledge.

Mayhew, P., Elliott, D. and Dowds, L. (1989). *The 1988 British Crime Survey*. London: HMSO.

Maxim, P. S. (1985). 'Cohort size and juvenile deliquency: a test of the Easterlin hypothesis' *Social Forces* vol 63, no. 3, pp. 661–681.

Maxim, P. S. (1985). 'Cohort size and juvenile deliquency in England and Wales' *Journal of Criminal Justice* vol 14, no. 6, pp. 491–499.

Orsagh, T. and Witte, A. D. (1981). 'Economic status and crime: implications for offender rehabilitation'. *Journal of Criminal Law and Criminology* vol 72, no. 3, pp. 1055–1071.

Poletti, F. (1882). *Del sentimento nella scienza del diritto penale* cited in Vold (op cit).

Radzinowicz, L. (1971). 'Economic pressures' in Radzinowicz, L. and Wolfgang, M. (Eds.), *Crime and Justice* vol 1, London: Basic Books.

Ramsey, J. B. (1969). 'Test for specification errors in classical linear least squares regression analysis' *Journal of the Royal Statistical Society* vol 31, pp. 350–371.

Sabol, W. J. (1989). 'The dynamics of unemployment and imprisonment in England and Wales, 1946–1985' *Criminology* vol 5, no. 2, pp. 147–168.

Spanos, A. (1986). *Statistical Foundations of Econometric Modelling* Cambridge: Cambridge University Press.

Tarling, R. (1982). 'Unemployment and Crime'. *Home Office Research Bulletin*. 14, pp. 28–33.

Thomas, D. A. (1925). *Social Aspects of the Business Cycle* London: Routledge.

Van Dijk, J. J. M., Mayhew, P. and Killias, M. (1990). *Experiences of Crime across the World: Key findings from the 1989 International Crime Survey*.

Vold, G. B. (1958). *Theoretical Criminology* New York: Oxford University Press.

Von Mayr (1867). 'Statistik der gerichtlichen Polizei im Konigreiche Bayern', cited in Mannheim (op. cit.)

Wilkins, L. (1964). *Social Deviance* London: Tavistock.

Wolpin, K. I. (1978). 'An economic analysis of crime and punishment in England and Wales 1894–1967' *Journal of Political Economy* vol. 86, 5, pp. 815–40.

Zellner, A. (1962). 'An efficient method of estimating seemingly unrelated regressions and tests of aggregation bias' *Journal of the American Statistical Association* vol 57, pp. 348–368.

Publications

Titles already published for the Home Office

Studies in the Causes of Delinquency and the Treatment of Offenders (SCDTO)

1. Prediction methods in relation to borstal training. Hermann Mannheim and Leslie T. Wilkins. 1955. viii + 276pp. (11 340051 9).
2. Time spent awaiting trial. Evelyn Gibson. 1960. v + 45pp. (34-368-2).
3. *Delinquent generations. Leslie T. Wilkins. 1960. iv + 20pp. (11 340053 5).
4. *Murder. Evelyn Gibson and S. Klein. 1961. iv + 44pp. (11 340054 3).
5. Persistent criminals. A study of all offenders liable to preventive detention in 1956. W. H. Hammond and Edna Chayen. 1963. ix + 237pp. (34-368-5).
6. *Some statistical and other numerical techniques for classifying individuals. P. McNaughton-Smith. 1965. v + 33pp. (34-368-6).
7. Probation research: a preliminary report. Part I. General outline of research. Part II. Study of Middlesex probation area (SOMPA). Steven Folkard, Kate Lyon, Margaret M. Carver and Erica O'Leary. 1966. vi + 58pp. (11 340374 7).
8. *Probation research: national study of probation. Trends and regional comparisions in probation (England and Wales). Hugh Barr and Erica O'Leary. 1966. vii + 51pp. (34-368-8).
9. *Probation research: A survey of group work in the probation service. Hugh Barr. 1966. vii + 94pp. (34-368-9).
10. *Types of delinquency and home background. A validation study of Hewitt and Jenkins' hypothesis. Elizabeth Field 1967. vi + 21pp. (34-368-10).
11. *Studies of female offenders. No. 1–Girls of 16-20 years sentenced to borstal or detention centre training in 1963. No. 2–Women offenders in the Metropolitan Police District in March and April 1957. No. 3–A description of women in prison on January 1, 1965. Nancy Goodman and Jean Price. 1967. v + 78pp. (34-368-11).
12. *The use of the Jesness Inventory on as sample of British probationers. Martin Davies. 1967. iv + 20pp. (34-368-12).
13. *The Jesness Inventory: application to approved school boys. Joy Mott. 1969. iv + 27pp. (11 340063 2).

Home Office Research Studies (HORS)

1. *Workloads in children's departments. Eleanor Grey. 1969. vi + 75pp. (11 340101 9).
2. *Probationers in their social environment. A study of male probationers aged 17-20, together with an analysis of those reconvicted within twelve months. Martin Davies. 1969. vii + 204pp. (11 340102 7).
3. *Murder 1957 to 1968. A Home Office Statistical Division report on murder in England and Wales. Evelyn Gibson and S. Klein (with annex by the Scottish Home and Health Department on murder in Scotland). 1969. vi + 94pp. (11 340103 5).
4. Firearms in crime. A Home Office Statistical Division report on indictable offences involving firearms in England and Wales. A. D. Weatherhead and B. M. Robinson. 1979. viii + 39pp. (11 340104 3).
5. *Financial penalties and probation. Martin Davies. 1970. vii + 39pp. (11 340105 1).
6. *Hostels for probationers. A study of the aims, working and variations in effectiveness of male probation hostels with special reference to the influence of the environment on delinquency. Ian Sinclair. 1971. ix + 200pp. (11 340106 X).

---

* Out of Print

PUBLICATIONS

7. *Prediction methods in criminology–including a prediction study of young men on probation. Frances H. Simon. 1971. xi + 234pp. (11 340107 8).
8. *Study of the juvenile liaison scheme in West Ham 1961-65. Marilyn Taylor. 1971. vi + 46pp. (11 340108 6).
9. *Explorations in after-care. I–After-care units London, Liverpool and Manchester. Martin Silberman (Royal London Prisoners' Aid Society) and Brenda Chapman. II–After-care hostels receiving a Home Office grant. Ian Sinclair and David Snow (HORU). III–St. Martin of Tours House, Aryeh Leissner (National Bureau for Co-operation in Child Care). 1971. xi + 140pp. (11 340109 4).
10. A survey of adoption in Great Britain. Eleanor Grey in collaboration with Ronald M. Blunden. 1971. ix + 168pp. (11 340110 8).
11. *Thirteen-year-old approved school boys in 1962s. Elizabeth Field, W. H. Hammond and J. Tizard. 1971. ix + 46pp. (11 340111 6).
12. Absconding from approved schools. R. V. G. Clarke and D. N. Martin 1971. vi + 146pp. (11 340112 4).
13. An experiment in personality assessment of young men remanded in custody. H. Sylvia Anthony. 1972. viii + 79pp. (11 340113 2).
14. *Girl offenders aged 17-20 years. I–Statistics relating to girl offenders aged 17-20 years from 1960 to 1970. II–Re-offending by girls released from borstal or detention centre training. III–The problems of girls released from borstal training during their period on after-care. Jean Davies and Nancy Goodman. 1972. v + 77pp. (11 340114 0).
15. *The controlled trial in institutional research-paradigm or pitfall for penal evaluators? R. V. G. Clarke and D. B. Cornish. 1972. v + 33pp. (11 340115 9).
16. *A survey of fine enforcement. Paul Softley. 1973. v + 65pp. (11 340116 7).
17. *An index of social environment-designed for use in social work menum research. Martin Davies. 1973. vi + 63pp. (11 340117 5).
18. *Social enquiry reports and the probation service. Martin Davies and Andrea Knopf. 1973. v + 49pp. (11 340118 3).
19. *Depression, psychopathic personality and attempted suicide in a borstal sample. H. Sylvia Anthony. 1973. viii + 44pp. (0 11 340119 1).
20. *The use of bail and custody by London magistrates' courts before and after the Criminal Justice Act 1967. Frances Simon and Mollie Weatheritt. 1974. vi + 78pp. (0 11 340120 5).
21. *Social work in the environment. A study of one aspect of probation practice. Martin Davies, with Margaret Rayfield, Alaster Calder and Tony Fowles. 1974. ix + 151pp. (0 11 340121 3).
22. Social work in prison. An experiment in the use of extended contact with offenders. Margaret Shaw. 1974. viii + 154pp. (11 340122 1).
23. Deliquency amongst opiate users. Joy Mott and Marilyn Taylor. 1974. vi + 31pp. (0 11 340663 0).
24. IMPACT. Intensive matched probation and after-care treatment Vol I-The design of the probation experiment and an interim evaluation. M. S. Folkard, A. J. Fowles, B. C. McWilliams, W. McWilliams, D. D. Smith, D. E. Smith and G. R. Walmsley. 1974. v + 54pp. (0 11 340664 9).
25. The approved school experience. An account of boys' experience of training under differing regimes of approved schools, with an attempt to evaluate the effectiveness of that training. Anne B. Dunlop. 1974. vii + 124pp. (0 11 340665 7).
26. *Absconding from open prisons. Charlotte Banks, Patricia Mayhew and R. J. Sapsford. 1975. viii + 89pp. (0 11 340666 5).
27. Driving while disqualified. Sue Kriefman. 1975. vi + 136pp. (0 11 340667 3).
28. Some male offenders' problems. I–Homeless offenders in Liverpool. W. McWilliams. II–Casework with short-term prisoners. Julie Holborn. 1975. x + 147pp. (0 11 340668 1).
29. *Community service orders. K. Pease, P. Durkin, D. Payne and J. Thorpe. 1975. viii + 80pp. (0 11 340669 X).
30. Field Wing Bail Hostel: the first nine months. Frances Simon and Sheena Wilson. 1975. viii + 55pp. (0 11 340670 3).

---

* Out of Print

TRENDS IN CRIME AND THEIR INTERPRETATION

31. Homicide in England and Wales 1967-71. Evelyn Gibson. 1975. iv + 59pp. (0 11 340753 X).
32. Residential treatment and its effects on delinquency. D. B. Cornish and R. V. G. Clarke. 1975. vi + 74pp. (0 11 340672 X).
33. Further studies of female offenders. Part A: Borstal girls eight years after release. Nancy Goodman, Elizabeth Maloney and Jean Davies. Part B: The sentencing of women at the London Higher Courts. Nancy Goodman, Paul Durkin and Janet Halton. Part C: Girls appearing before a juvenile court. Jean Davies. 1976. vi + 114pp. (0 11 340673 8).
34. *Crime as opportunity. P. Mayhew, R. V. G. Clarke, A. Sturman and J. M. Hough. 1976. vii + 36pp. (11 340674 6).
35. The effectiveness of sentencing: a review of the literature. S. R. Brody. 1976. v + 89pp. (0 11 340675 4).
36. IMPACT. Intensive matched probation and after-care treatment. Vol. II–The results of the experiment. M. S. Folkard, D. E. Smith and D. D. 1976. xi + 40pp. (0 11 340676 2).
37. Police cautioning in England and Wales. J. A. Ditchfield. 1976. v + 31pp. (0 11 340677 0).
38. Parole in England and Wales. C. P. Nuttall, with E. E. Barnard, A. J. Fowles, A. Frost, W. H. Hammond, P. Mayhew, K. Pease, R. Tarling and M. J. Weatheritt 1977. vi + 90pp. (0 11 340678 9).
39. Community service assessed in 1976. K. Pease, S. Billingham and I. Earnshaw. 1977. vi + 29pp. (0 11 340679 7).
40. Screen violence and film censorship: a review of research. Stephen Brody. 1977. vii + 179pp. (0 11 340680 0).
41. *Absconding from borstals. Gloria K. Laycock. 1977. v + 82pp. (0 11 340681 9).
42. Gambling: a review of the literature and its implications for policy and research. D. B. Cornish. 1978. xii + 284pp. (0 11 340682 7).
43. Compensation orders in magistrates' courts. Paul Softley. 1978. v + 41pp. (0 11 340683 5).
44. Research in criminal justice. John Croft. 1978. iv + 16pp. (0 11 340684 3).
45. Prison welfare: an account of an experiment at Liverpool. A. J. Fowles. 1978. v + 34pp. (0 11 340685 1).
46. Fines in magistrates' courts. Paul Softley. 1978. v + 42pp. (0 11 340686 X).
47. Tackling vandalism. R. V. G. Clarke (editor), F. J. Gladstone, A. Sturman and Sheena Wilson (contributors). 1978. vi + 91pp. (0 11 340687 8).
48. Social inquiry reports: a survey. Jennifer Thorpe. 1979. vi + 55pp. (0 11 340688 6).
49. Crime in public view. P. Mayhew, R. V. G. Clarke, J. N. Burrows, J. M. Hough and S. W. C. Winchester. 1979. v + 36pp. (0 11 340689 4).
50. *Crime and the community. John Croft. 1979. v + 16pp. (0 11 340690 8).
51. Life-sentence prisoners. David Smith (editor), Christopher Brown, Joan Worth, Roger Sapsford and Charlotte Banks (contributors). 1979. iv + 51pp. (0 11 340691 6).
52. Hostels for offenders. Jane E. Andrews, with an appendix by Bill Sheppard. 1979. v + 30pp. (0 11 340692 4).
53. Previous convictions, sentence and reconviction: a statistical study of a sample of 5,000 offenders convicted in January 1971. G. J. O. Phillpotts and L. B. Lancucki. 1979. v + 55pp. (0 11 340693 2).
54. Sexual offences, consent and sentencing. Roy Walmsley and Karen White. 1979. vi + 77pp. (0 11 340694 0).
55. Crime prevention and the police. John Burrows, Paul Ekblom and Kevin Heal. 1979. v + 37pp. (0 11 340695 9).
56. Sentencing practice in magistrates' courts. Roger Tarling, with the assistance of Mollie Weatheritt. 1979. vii + 54pp. (0 11 340696 7).
57. Crime and comparative research. John Croft. 1979. iv + 16pp. (0 11 340697 5).
58. Race, crime and arrests. Philip Stevens and Carole F. Willis. 1979. v + 69pp. (0 11 340698 3).
59. Research and criminal policy. John Croft. 1980. iv + 14pp. (0 11 340699 1).
60. Junior attendance centres. Anne B. Dunlop. 1980. v + 47pp. (0 11 340700 9).
61. Police interrogation: an observational study in four police stations. Paul Softley, with the assistance of David Brown, Bob Forde, George Mair and David Moxon. 1980. vii + 67pp. (0 11 340701 7).

---

* Out of Print

PUBLICATIONS

62. Co-ordinating crime prevention efforts. F. J. Gladstone. 1980. v + 74pp. (0 11 340702 5).
63. Crime prevention publicity: an assessment. D. Riley and P. Mayhew. 1980. v + 47pp. (0 11 340703 3).
64. Taking offenders out of circulation. Stephen Brody and Roger Tarling. 1980. v + 46pp. (0 11 340704 1).
65. *Alcoholism and social policy: are we on the right lines? Mary Tuck. 1980. v + 30pp. (0 11 340705 X).
66. Persistent petty offenders. Suzan Fairhead. 1981. vi + 78pp. (0 11 340706 8).
67. Crime control and the police. Pauline Morris and Kevin Heal. 1981. v + 71pp. (0 11 340707 6).
68. Ethnic minorities in Britain: a study of trends in their position since 1961. Simon Field, George Mair, Tom Rees and Philip Stevens. 1981. v + 48pp. (0 11 340708 4).
69. Managing criminological research. John Croft. 1981. iv + 17pp. (0 11 340709 2).
70. Ethinic minorities, crime and policing: a survey of the experiences of West Indians and whites. Mary Tuck and Peter Southgate. 1981. iv + 54pp. (0 11 340765 3).
71. Contested trials in magistrate's courts. Julie Vennard. 1982. v + 32pp. (0 11 340766 1).
72. Pulic disorder: a review of research and a study in one inner city area. Simon Field and Peter Southgate. 1982. v + 77pp. (0 11 340767 X).
73. Clearing up crime. John Burrows and Roger Tarling. 1981. vii + 31pp. (0 11 340768 8).
74. Residential burglary: the limits of prevention. Stuart Winchester and Hilary Jackson. 1982. v + 47pp. (0 11 340769 6).
75. Concerning crime. John Croft. 1982. iv + 16pp. (0 11 340770 X).
76. The British Crime Survey: first report. Mike Hough and Pat Mayhew. 1983. v + 62pp. (0 11 340786 6).
77. Contacts between police and public: findings from the British Crime Survey. Peter Southgate and Paul Ekblom. 1984. v + 42pp. (0 11 340771 8).
78. Fear of crime in England and Wales. Michael Maxfield. 1984. v + 57pp. (0 11 340772 6).
79. Crime and police effectiveness. Ronald V Clarke and Mike Hough 1984. iv + 33pp. (0 11 340773 3).
80. The attitudes of ethnic minorities. Simon Field. 1984. v + 49pp. (0 11 340774 2).
81. Victims of crime: the dimensions of risk. Michael Gottfredson. 1984. v + 54p. (0 11 340775 0).
82. The tape recording of police interviews with suspects: an interim report. Carole Willis. 1984. v + 45pp. (0 11 340776 9).
83. Parental supervision and juvenile delinquency. David Riley and Margaret Shaw. 1985. v + 90pp. (0 11 340799 8).
84. Adult prisons and prisoners in England and Wales 1970-1982: a review of the findings of social research. Joy Mott. 1985. vi + 73pp. (0 11 340801 3).
85. Taking account of crime: key findings from the 1984 British Crime Survey. Mike Hough and Pat Mayhew. 1985. vi + 115pp. (0 11 341801 2).
86. Implementing crime prevention measures. Tim Hope. 1985. vi + 82pp. (0 11 340812 9).
87. Resettling refugees. the lessons of research. Simon Field. 1985. vi + 66pp. (0 11 340815 3).
88. Investigating burglary: the measurement of police performance. John Burrows. 1986. vi + 36pp. (0 11 340824 2).
89. Personal violence. Roy Walmsley. 1986. vi + 87pp. (0 11 340827 7).
90. Police-public encounters. Peter Southgate. 1986. vi + 150pp. (0 11 340834 X).
91. Grievance procedures in prisons. John Ditchfield and Claire Austin. 1986. vi + 87pp. (0 11 340839 0).
92. The effectiveness of the Forensic Science Service. Malcolm Ramsay. 1987. v + 100pp. (0 11 340842 0).
93. The police complaints procedure: a survey of complainant's views. David Brown. 1987. v + 98pp. (0 11 340853 6).
94. The validity of the reconviction prediction score. Denis Ward. 1987. vi + 46pp. (0 11 340882 X).
95. Economic aspects of the illicit drug market enforcement policies in the United Kingdom. Adam Wagstaff and Alan Maynard. 1988. vii + 156pp. (0 11 340883 8).

* Out of Print

96. Schools, disruptive behaviour and delinquency: a review of literature. John Graham. 1988. v + 70pp. (0 11 340887 0).
97. The tape recording of police interviews with suspects: a second interim report. Carole Willis, John Macleod and Peter Naish. 1988. vii + 97pp. (0 11 340890 0).
98. Triable-either-way cases: Crown Court or magistrate's court. David Riley and Julie Vennard. 1988. v + 52pp. (0 11 340891 9).
99. Directing patrol work: a study of uniformed policing. John Burrows and Helen Lewis. 1988 v + 66pp. (0 11 340891 9).
100. Probation day centres. George Mair. 1988. v + 44pp. (0 11 340894 3).
101. Amusement machines: dependency and delinquency. John Graham. 1988. v + 48pp. (0 11 340895 1).
102. The use and enforcement of compensation orders in magistrates' courts. Tim Newburn. 1988. v + 49pp. (0 11 340896 X).
103. Sentencing practice in the Crown Court. David Moxon. 1988. v + 90pp. (0 11 340902 8).
104. Detention at the police station under the Police and Criminal Evidence Act 1984. David Brown. 1988. v + 88pp. (0 11 340908 7).
105. Changes in rape offences and sentencing. Charles Lloyd and Roy Walmsley. 1989. vi + 53pp. (0 11 340910 9).
106. Concerns about rape. Lorna Smith. 1989. v + 48pp. (0 11 340911 7).
107. Domestic violence. Lorna Smith. 1989. v + 132pp. (0 11 340925 7).
108. Drinking and disorder: a study of non-metropolitan violence. Mary Tuck. 1989. v + 111pp. (0 11 340926 5).
109. Special security units. Roy Walmsley. 1989. v + 114pp. (0 11 340961 3).
110. Pre-trial delay: the implications of time limits. Patricia Morgan and Julie Vennard. 1989. v + 66pp. (0 11 340964 8).
111. The 1988 British Crime Survey. Pat Mayhew, David Elliott and Lizanne Dowds. 1989. v + 133pp. (0 11 340965 6).
112. The settlement of claims at the Criminal Injuries Compensation Board. Tim Newburn. 1989. v + 40pp. (0 11 340967 2).
113. Race, community groups and service delivery. Hilary Jackson and Simon Field. 1989. v + 62pp. (0 11 340972 9).
114. Money payment supervision orders: probation policy and practice. George Mair and Charles Lloyd. 1989. v + 40pp. (0 11 340971 0).
115. Suicide and self-injury in prison: a literature review. Charles Lloyd. 1990. v + 69pp. (0 11 340974 5).
116. Keeping in Touch: police-victim communication in two areas. Tim Newburn and Susan Merry. 1990. v + 52pp. (0 11 340974 5).

ALSO

Designing out crime. R. V. G. Clarke and P. Mayhew (editors). 1980. viii + 186pp. (0 11 340732 7).
(This book collects, with an introduction, studies that were originally published in HORS 34, 47, 49, 55 62 and 63 and which are illustrative of the 'situational' approach to crime prevention.)

Policing today. Kevin Heal, Roger Tarling and John Burrows (editors). v + 181pp. (0 11 340800 5).
(This books brings together twelve separate studies on police matters produced during the last few years by the Unit. The collection records some relatively little known contribution to the debate on policing.)

Managing Criminal Justice: a collection of papers. David Moxon (ed.). 1985. vi + 222pp. (0 11 340811 0).
(This book brings together a number of studies bearing on the management of the criminal justice system. It includes papers by social scientists and operational researchers working within the Research and Planning Unit, and academic researchers who have studied particular aspects of the criminal process.)

Situational Crime Prevention: from theory into practice. Kevin Heal and Gloria Laycock (editors). 1986. vii + 166pp. (0 11 340826 9).

PUBLICATIONS

(Following the publication of *Designing Out Crime*, further research has been completed on the theoretical background to crime prevention. In drawing this work together this book sets down some of the theoretical concerns and discusses the emerging practical issues. It includes contributions by Unit staff as well as academics from this country and abroad.)

Communities and crime reduction. Tim Hope and Margaret Shaw (eds.). 1988. vii + 311pp. (11 340892 7).

(The central theme of this book is the possibility of preventing crime by building upon the resources of local communities and of active citizens. The specially commissioned chapters, by distinguished international authors, review contemporary research and policy on community crime prevention.)

New directions in police training. Peter Southgate (ed.). 1988. xi + 256pp. (11 340889 7).

(Training is central to the development of the police role, and particular thought and effort now go into making it more responsive current needs — in order to produce police officers who are are both effective and sensitive in their dealing with the public. This book illustrates some of the thinking and research behind these developments.)

The above HMSO publications can be purchased from Government Bookshops or through booksellers.

The following Home Office research publications are available on request from the Home Office Research and Planning Unit, 50 Queen Anne's Gate, London SW1H 9AT.

Research Unit Papers (RUP)

1. Uniformed police work and management technology. J. M. Hough. 1980.
2. Supplementary information on sexual offences and sentencing. Roy Walmsley and Karen White. 1980.
3. Board of visitor adjudications. David Smith, Claire Austin and John Ditchfield. 1981.
4. Day centres and probation. Susan Fairhead, with the assistance of J. Wilkinson-Grey. 1981.

Research and Planning Unit Papers (RPUP)

5. Ethnic minorities and complaints against the police. Philip Stevens and Carole Willis. 1982.
6. *Crime and public housing. Mike Hough and Pat Mayhew (editors). 1982.
7. *Abstracts of race relations research. George Mair and Philip Stevens (editors). 1982.
8. Police probationer training in race relations. Peter Southgate. 1982.
9. *The police response to calls from the public. Paul Ekblom and Kevin Heal. 1982.
10. City centre crime: a situational approach to prevention. Malcolm Ramsay. 1982.
11. Burglary in schools: the prospects for prevention. Tim Hope. 1982.
12. *Fine enforcement. Paul Softley and David Moxon. 1982.
13. Vietnamese refugees. Peter Jones. 1982.
14. Community resources for victims of crime. Karen Williams. 1983.
15. The use, effectiveness and impact of police stop and search powers. Carole Willis. 1983.
16. Acquittal rates. Sid Butler. 1983.
17. Criminal justice comparisons: the case of Scotland and England and Wales. Lorna J. F. Smith. 1983.
18. Time taken to deal with juveniles under criminal proceedings. Catherine Frankenburg and Roger Tarling. 1983.
19. Civilian review of complaints against the police: a survey of the United States literature. David C. Brown. 1983.
20. Police action on motoring offences. David Riley. 1983.
21. *Diverting drunks from the criminal justice system. Sue Kingsley and George Mair. 1983.
22. The staff resource implications of an independent prosecution system. Peter R. Jones. 1983.
23. Reducing the prison population: an exploratory study in Hampshire. David Smith, Bill Sheppard, George Mair, Karen Williams. 1984.

---

* Out of Print

TRENDS IN CRIME AND THEIR INTERPRETATION

24. Criminal justice system model: magistrates' courts sub-model. Susan Rice. 1984.
25. Measures of police effectiveness and efficiency. Ian Sinclair and Clive Miller. 1984.
26. Punishment practice by prison Boards of Visitors. Susan Iles, Adrienne Connors, Chris May, Joy Mott. 1984.
27. *Reparation, conciliation and mediation: current projects and plans in England and Wales. Tony Marshall. 1984.
28. Magistrates' domestic courts: new perspectives. Tony Marshall (editor). 1984.
29. Racism awareness training for the police. Peter Southgate. 1984.
30. Community constables: a study of a policing initiative. David Brown and Susan Iles. 1985.
31. Recruiting volunteers. Hilary Jackson. 1985.
32. Juvenile sentencing: is there a tariff? David Moxon, Peter Jones, Roger Tarling. 1985.
33. Bringing people together: mediation and reparation projects in Great Britain. Tony Marshall and Martin Walpole. 1985.
34. Remands in the absence of the accused. Chris May. 1985.
35. Modelling the criminal justice system. Patricia M. Morgan. 1985.
36. The criminal justice system model: the flow model. Hugh Pullinger. 1986.
37. Burglary: police actions and victim views. John Burrows. 1986.
38. Unlocking community resources: four experimental government small grants schemes. Hilary Jackson. 1986.
39. The cost of discriminating: a review of the literature. Shirley Dex. 1986.
40. Waiting for Crown Court trial: the remand population. Rachel Pearce. 1987.
41. Children's evidence the need for corroboration. Carol Hedderman. 1987.
42. A preliminary study of victim offender mediation and reparation schemes in England & Wales. Gwynn Davis, Jacky Boucherat, David Watson, Adrian Thatcher (Consultant). 1987.
43. Explaining fear of crime: evidence from the 1984 British Crime Survey. Michael Maxfield. 1987.
44. Judgements of crime seriousness: evidence from the 1984 British Crime Survey. Ken Pease. 1988.
45. Waiting time on the day in magistrates' courts: a review of case listings practices. David Moxon and Roger Tarling (editors). 1988.
46. Bail and probation work: the ILPS temporary bail action project. George Mair. 1988.
47. Police work and manpower allocation. Roger Tarling. 1988.
48. Computers in the courtroom. Carol Hedderman. 1988.
49. Data interchange between magistrates' courts and other agencies. Carol Hedderman. 1988.
50. Bail and probation work II: the use of London probation bail hostels for bailees. Helen Lewis and George Mair. 1989.
51. The role and function of police community liaison officers. Susan V. Phillips and Raymond Cochrane. 1989.
52. Insuring against burglary losses. Helen Lewis. 1989.
53. Remand decisions in Brighton and Bournemouth. Patricia Morgan and Rachel Pearce. 1989.
54. Racially motivated incidents reported to the police. Jayne Seagrave. 1989.
55. Review of research on re-offending of mentally disordered offenders. David J. Murray. 1990.
56. Risk prediction and probation: papers from a Research and Planning Unit workshop. George Mair (editor). 1990.

Research Bulletin

The Research Bulletin is published twice a year and consists mainly of short articles relating to projects which are part of the Home Office Research and Planning Unit's research programme.

---

* Out of Print